WHAT OTHERS ARE SAYING

Emily takes us on a journey through self-doubt, pain, and, ultimately, redemption. I thought about her story for days after finishing it, ever reminded that each person carries bruises and walks a long road to reach self-discovery and self-love.

—Sherrean
Dean of career technical education,
Gavilan College

This is a story of perseverance. Somehow, in some way, Emily knew she was capable of more—that there was something better for her. We must love ourselves enough to be loved by others and to love others. Taking care of ourselves is the best gift we give others. Emily, you have more strength and resolve than you realize. You're an inspiration.

—Barbara
Good friend

Thank you for sharing your story. I am so happy that you completed your project, to be free, and having the faith you have always had. Emily's story will be helpful and empowering to women. Violence is not okay. With great respect and love, your friend.

—Debbie Ruiz
Community Solutions

Wow! Wow! With this book you have given me a new life. You have helped me see all that has happened in my own journey. Everyone that has passed in and out of my life was there for so many reasons, whether to help them or to help me. I will look at my life differently and know that every morning God has a greater plan for me. I love you, and I am so proud to be shoulder to shoulder with you.

—Sally Brown
Cousin

Free at Last

THE STRUGGLE

TO BE GOOD ENOUGH

Many of us live with unbearable thought of feeling there is "no way out".

Free at Last
THE STRUGGLE
TO BE GOOD ENOUGH

I. M. DAUNTLESS
Chapter Zero Poetry By Jay Steel

TATE PUBLISHING
AND ENTERPRISES, LLC

Published by Tate Publishing & Enterprises, LLC
127 E. Trade Center Terrace | Mustang, Oklahoma 73064 USA
1.888.361.9473 | www.tatepublishing.com

Tate Publishing is committed to excellence in the publishing industry. The company reflects the philosophy established by the founders, based on Psalm 68:11,
"The Lord gave the word and great was the company of those who published it."

Book design copyright © 2015 by Tate Publishing, LLC. All rights reserved.
Cover design by Samson Lim
Interior design by Jomar Ouano

Published in the United States of America

ISBN: 978-1-68237-378-1
Religion / Christian Life / Inspirational
15.09.25

To my lovely daughters, thank you both
for loving me unconditionally

Acknowledgments

Thank you to my mom and dad, who loved me and supported me through my good and bad journeys, especially my education.

Thank you, Sister and Brother, for also being in my life. I know I was difficult to understand.

I would like to thank my brother-in-law Jason Mallory. Without his guidance and experience, this task of publishing would have been a little more difficult.

Thank you to the many people who believed in me no matter where I was or how I was doing. You and your prayers have helped me to become the woman I am today.

Thank you to my therapist, counselors, teachers, first responders, and Community Solutions. Your organization does wonderful work.

Contents

INTRODUCTION

A Question of Forgiveness

How do we move on and have a feeling of purpose especially after experiencing trauma in a way we believe no one else would ever be able to relate?

Have you ever had a feeling of being stuck, of not being worthy, or having the thought that since these were my choices, is this possibly all there is for me?

Could it be forgiveness; could that be the key? If it is a solution, then how do we take the steps to implement it? What is your definition of true forgiveness? Each of us has our own ability and level we think is comfortable, but is it always the right way just because we are comfortable?

According to a dictionary I picked up, the definition of *forgiveness* is, "to grant pardon for; or remission of, to absolve; to give up all claim on account of; to grant pardon to (a person, or action); to cease to feel resentment against." Synonyms for this word include *excuse, absolve,* and *acquit.*

The definition of *unforgiving* is "not willing to forgive, unmerciful." Not forgiving can sometimes give permission to the blocking of incidents, people, and places that have caused us pain when remembered. For me, it meant the inability to move on.

I personally have experienced the feeling of being stuck, the feeling of being squashed and smothered, and experienced the inability to see through the blur. This blur can be foggy and gray. I have gone about my day and sometimes wondered how I even got from one place to another. Friends, this blur can be dangerous; please find someone to talk to. Do not allow it to take over your life.

Many of you may have had these types of feelings throughout different situations in your life like in school, relationships, finances, work, and home. It is a very real feeling.

If being stuck is related to not forgiving, then how do we forgive others, or even better, how do we forgive ourselves in order to move on and see over the blur?

I believe forgiving ourselves can be the most difficult thing to do at times and may even seem impossible. This has at times kept me bound in chains. The links filled with the notion of not feeling worthy or deserving—the feeling of not being able to move.

Could the result of our consequences be our fate?

Some of us have hated and continue to carry the ugliness of vengeance, which can linger from the abuse and the thought of unspeakable crimes poured upon us.

Many of us live with the unbearable thought of feeling there is no way out.

Well, there is a way out, and this is a story of how a young girl, who became a woman, overcame some of the weakest moments in her life.

> I will sing to the Lord because he has been so good to me. (Psalm 13:6)

1

Emily

My story begins with a young lady named Emily, who has mesmerized me with her strength and fire-eating courage. Emily is a beautiful woman who I met a few years ago. She is bright, caring, loving, and openly shares her testimony to others. She has dark hair, large brown eyes, and a smile that brightens your heart. When you meet her, you would only know that she has a deep love for the Lord and that she is openly leaning on the Lord for her strength.

She shares her life and her pains, not in a bragging kind of way, but in a way that would let you know she truly can relate to your pains. Emily is a single parent who decided it was going to be best to go to college to support her family. Her story of survival through many heartaches inspired me to write and introduce her to you, my reader. Her many struggles reminded me of so many different times I had made the same mistakes. The most inspiring thing I see is her faith, her desire to keep moving forward, no matter what gets in her way.

Emily, it is all yours:

Thank you, dear author, and thank you for taking the time to allow me to share my story. As a small child, I always knew there was a God. I recall many moments looking into the sky and talking to the stars. I just did not know that I could really know Him. There is not much of my childhood that I can recall, only short moments and some incidences or outings.

My mother was busied about the house with three children. I was the eldest of the three.

I had a rough time growing up and always felt alone but did not understand why. Our family attended a Catholic church regularly on Sundays, offering our $1.00 as the basket came by. We attended classes to partake in the preparation of our first Holy Communion. Mass was at church on Sundays, although I do not recall it ever being within our home from Monday to Saturday.

My mother dressed my sister and me as though we were twins. My mother told me recently that she had always wanted twins, and since we were so close in size and age, this was going to be the closest to having what she wanted for the short time while we were small. This would be an easy task while we were small, but as we grew older and began to have our own identity, we gradually began to dress as we chose. My brother was the middle child. He enjoyed playing by himself although most of the time we played together.

My mother, who was and is still very beautiful, did not drive until I was eight or nine years old. We walked everywhere, sometimes borrowing the shopping cart in order to carry us or the groceries purchased. This must have been a difficult task. My father, who was and is still a handsome man, worked many hours and was gone most of the day. He worked in retail, and for those of you who know, as a manager, a normal workweek can be as many as sixty hours a week.

It seemed as though we had a pretty good lifestyle financially. We were a part of an upper-class neighborhood with a rather large home that my parents owned. This was unusual within our Hispanic culture, especially in the area we lived, although I really did not know what the word *Hispanic* was at the time. As children, we did not know the difference; we were close to our neighborhood families and played regularly with them.

As a young child, I recall having a lot of imagination. The neighborhood kids and I would do different things as young entrepreneurs to raise money. We orchestrated short plays and skating shows for the families. This was a lot of fun. Our family was blessed with a large home and yard. We had a lot of fruit trees on our property, and in the spring I recall asking our mother if we could sell fruit with the wagon. I had fun doing that. It was also a way to get the trees pruned of fruit—very creative on my mother's part.

My parents worked very hard to give us a good upbringing. I am not sure how it happens with some of us, maybe you can relate. I lost the feeling of knowing who I truly was and where my heritage and culture was from. People in our circle of friends did not talk much about being Mexican and Hispanic or where our heritage came from. I eventually felt as though I was the black sheep of the family. I had a difficult time living this way in what I believed was an unreal lifestyle. I think this may have been the beginning signs of my childhood depression.

My mother and father did not speak Spanish in front of us as it was not normal in our neighborhood. I was the dark-skinned child; I even recall not being able to be in the sun too much because I would get too dark. I still get very dark! But now it is my choice.

All I wanted as a child and young lady growing up was someone to hold me, hug me, and love me. My mother had little time to be affectionate; she did not have good examples in her home as a child growing up and recently told me she has always had a difficult time with affection. She had three little ones running and playing all day. There was also the tending to my father's regimen as to how things in his mind should be. She once shared with me that my father was very strict with her and told her he wanted us and the house clean before he arrived home. He required that we be dressed and sitting on the porch to welcome him. I always thought this was an exciting time. I loved getting dressed up to meet my father. For my mother, it was a stressful time as she hoped that she did not make a mistake and that we all looked presentable.

This was the beginning of the cycle of codependency, which I later found out would be a learned behavior for me.

2

First Painful Memories

My parents started to separate two to three times a year. Not legally, but my father would tell my mother he did not want to be married and he needed a break. My mother would take us by Greyhound bus or train to her parent's home, which was about a four-hour ride. Remember, she did not drive yet. She tried to make it a journey of sort—a vacation. I loved going at first; it was like a small adventure. My grandmother had this beautiful little room in their home. Candles, pictures of saints, rosaries, pictures of different family members that were being prayed for, and even a kneeling bench: it was like having her own Catholic church within her small home.

There were a set of stairs with a curtain that none of us were allowed to go up to. I surely did not want to.

The fun times were getting together with my cousins. We played a lot; all of us were about the same age. We had so much fun; I did not think of it as a sad thing but a fun time to visit. I was young, and we were on short adventures. My mother was one of eleven, so when we went to visit, many of the aunts and uncles would visit as well and bring their children for us to play together. We children would play outside with Grandfather while Grandmother was inside cooking with the aunts. Grandfather would entice us with money to buy candy. I recall one time that all of us around him; he asked me to sit on his lap. In those days, little girls wore dresses all the time.

My grandfather attempted to ride his hand up my dress and under my panties. I pushed his hand away and ran to play with my other cousins. I never told anyone. Why, I am not sure.

I am not quite sure when and how it happened, but one year, it just was not fun. The cousins did not come to play with us like before, and aunts and uncles did not come running when we arrived. When bedtime came, it was not fun at all. I am not sure how it started or why, but I would be asked to sleep with my grandparents. This was not a good time for me to remember. My grandfather slowly began touching me, and I was afraid to go to sleep. I can remember a time my grandmother was standing at the doorway looking in. I was confused and afraid, and this led to many years of sick and painful memories.

One day I asked my mother why one of my uncles and his kids did not come over any longer. It was just relayed that we did not need to know. Later I would find out the truth. His daughter had told him of the strange things my grandfather had done to her. He came and had a few harsh words with my grandfather—his father. My poor cousin and my uncle were banished from my mother's family. This estranged family relationship lasted over many years through adulthood. My cousin did the right thing by telling, and I am proud of her and how she has grown to be a beautiful, loving woman.

Today I am grateful to have a wonderful relationship with my uncle and his family. It is such a blessing to have them back in my life.

As we grew older, we were not required to go to visit as often, and finally the visits stopped altogether. I had channeled my resentment toward my mother. I guess I figured she should have known it was her father, but how could she? I had not talked to her about the things that had occurred during these visits.

When my grandfather died, my mother wanted me go to the services; I did not want to go. My father said I should in order to see that he was finally gone! It was so scary walking up to the coffin, but I did it. Remember, up to this point my mother had not known what had occurred.

In my mind I could sense my mother's embarrassment at the fact that I did not shed a tear and the fact that I did not want to attend. What were her family members going to say? They surely would talk about us after we left.

My mother told me recently that her family had told her the stories were lies, and she just had to believe them. She was doing the best she could to protect her own family. She did not want to believe it was true. Who would want to know this of their own father? I realize now she did the best she could.

It took many years for me to be able to understand and have a relationship with my mother only because I did not know how to love myself. I am so very grateful that I know the Lord now and that God has since graced me with lessons on forgiveness. Those lessons are not limited to me forgiving my mother; most importantly, they also include me asking for forgiveness *from* my mother.

3

Our Double Lives

Now as I begin this next chapter, remember please this is me, Emily, talking and writing. This is me and my accounts. Our brains are so unique. We store things within the same family circle and can recall them in front of each other, each with a different outcome. Try this with your families. Recall a memory and details, write them down, and then ask your siblings or family members to recall the same incident. They either do not remember the same incident or say, "It did not happen that way, let me tell you how it really happened." Right! Well with that in mind, here is the next chapter.

My father had many extramarital affairs, and for some reason, I was okay with this. This is how sick I was! I was an uncaring, selfish young girl who was full of pain. For most of my young adolescent years, I felt lost and hurt deep within the pits of my being. My mother told me that one day my father told her he was leaving and that she was crying and that she told me he was not coming back. She was angry and upset. She said that I went to my room and cried and cried and would not stop crying. She ended up having to call my father at one of his mistress's home and told him that I would not stop crying. He came home and comforted me, and that led to him making the decision of staying around at least until we were grown. The hurt and pain he had in seeing me this way burdened him for many years. This would be my first feeling of abandonment and my defining moment in realizing that I needed to work at keeping someone to stay with me, to love me, and I would go to any length to make him stay. I adopted this learned behavior later in life to make any man stay.

Now remember we lived as upper-class citizens for many years. This was now the only way my mother knew how to live. There was shame in what was going on because of the embarrassment and humiliation that my father caused her. How was she going to hide this from people? How was she ever going to live up to the standards she was so used to having?

Remember, my mother came from a Catholic family. There was no leaving or divorcing. In my eyes, it was an imaginative lifestyle that was so different behind closed doors. In front of their friends, there was never a sense that anything was wrong. I later found out that my poor mother had a lot of shame and humiliation that she felt my father caused. She had a long battle of hiding this from everyone. That would be a difficult job for anyone to do. My mother felt trapped, a feeling I later felt all too well. As I write this, I realize more than ever each of us comes from a family that closes the door, and maybe some of you have to live this type of double life. If you think it is not normal, listen to your heart; don't be afraid that you are questioning your own family. And please, if anyone is hurting you, please open the door! Let someone know.

My father was and is a loving, caring man. He just had issues with infidelity. He loved my mother, this I am sure of. He just had a difficult time settling down.

Today, after so many years, he realizes he cannot change the past, but now he has a belief and faith in Christ. He knows forgiveness is important and that he does not have to carry this shame any longer.

My mother—bless her heart—she did the best she could with everything she had in front of her. Not knowing how to forgive made her life difficult. She felt a lot of pain for many years.

The blessings I can share now are that both of them recently have decided to give it all to God and live a life that allows them to learn how to forgive with faith.

4

Encounter with the Black Book

My teenage years were filled with depression. I was always depressed, sad, and confused. I remember even having to go to the office to drink milk to calm my ulcers during elementary school. That would be a huge red flag in our time today. In those days, there were not any resources to address awareness for mental health issues, especially for children. Children are supposed to be happy, not depressed, right?

At the age of thirteen I tried to commit suicide to be closer to God. I didn't know Him yet but thought that by dying, I could be with Him right then and there. I took a bottle of aspirin. My father was home and knew something was wrong. I shared with him what I had done. He made sure I was okay, not needing medical attention; then he consoled me. My thought was that my mother was jealous of my relationship with my father. I thought she wanted me to hate him for what he was doing to her, but I could not. Remember, none of us knew how to forgive, only how to hide and shush.

My desire was to continue to have a relationship with my father. For some reason I figured he understood me more than my mother did. I did not fully understand my mother's pain. This was not fair in any way, I know now. My mother got dealt some pretty bad cards. She did the best she could with what she knew. She probably wanted the same thing as I did: to feel good enough and to be loved. There was nothing normal in her life at this time; it was just "let's survive and try to get through this day."

Our family moved to a small town. I was now fourteen. Ugh, how I hated moving in the middle of a school year! To start middle school in a new school was heartwrenching.

For those of you who have had to move a lot, I know you know this feeling oh so well.

As children, we really do not like it, okay? It is a very real pain. Please make sure that you comfort your children and work with them through this transition because it is a tough one. Eventually, I settled in. I met up with some kids who took me under their wings and introduced me to my first marijuana cigarette, or joint as we now know it. And so this was my first time learning how to self-medicate.

My parents owned their own business, and my father had the three of us children work for him in the family business. My father kept doing his thing: drinking, gambling, and all the things he was accustomed to doing. We lived a pretty decent lifestyle in a pretty nice neighborhood. Each one of us children had a different encounter with these teenage years. This story is only my account; my siblings may have a different account.

I continued through school with my new friends. I was a pretty smart young girl and had my basics down; I came from my past school with straight As. I definitely stood out among my friends; I had no idea what *street-smart* meant.

Soon I was getting in trouble for cutting class. I remember in high school begging my mom and dad to let me be in an outside program within the school, one that did not focus on the core curriculum. They thought I was crazy; so did my counselor.

Hey, I just referred to them as Mom and Dad, this is good! I think I will continue on with that!

Eventually they caved and gave me my way; the teacher knew I did not need to be there, but he welcomed me. Our school days were built on curriculum, learning basic social skills, and physical education. Softball was big! In those days, we were able to smoke on campus. They actually squared off this little grass-and-dirt area, and as long as we stood there while smoking, it was okay. Isn't that just crazy?

There were many days of drinking and carrying on during our school day.

My poor mom and dad; I was completely lost in finding my identity. They were working long hours, and by now my mom started driving and had a pretty good job downtown. There were some days that my friends and I would take off from school and go to my house to party. We watched the time and hid in the closet while my mom came home for her lunch hour.

That was a pretty funny sight; can you imagine all of us hiding in different closets throughout the house, trying to be very quiet? I was out of control.

I worked on most Saturdays for my dad at his business. I cannot remember the manager's name at the time, although he always had a big black book that he would read at his desk. One day I asked him about this big book.

"Emily," he said, "this is a Bible."

Hallelujah! My first encounter with God! The manager began to read scripture and bear witness to me about the love of Christ. I listened, and my heart was open. I started to look forward to coming to work on Saturdays now and to come listen about God's love. One day he talked to me about salvation. I recited the sinner's prayer with him and began my relationship with Christ. This was amazing; finally, I knew of a love so great and powerful. I was on fire for God and wanted to learn as much as I could. Things were finally making sense. I had a true friend, and I was beginning to learn about forgiveness. My new friend, the manager, did not stay much longer after that; he was not comfortable with my dad's lifestyle, and he had to tell me good-bye. I was sad, of course, but tried to understand.

Things were sent on a little whirlwind as I began my radical plight for Jesus. I wanted everyone to know. However,

I was one of those fear-factor kids, talking about the end of the world and people needing to repent (not that this isn't important). It is true stuff, only now I understand that love is the most important thing to remember about our relationship with Jesus. He wants to be our friend, our first, and our person on whom we rely.

Now remember I grew up in a Catholic home whose members no longer went to church. I am sure this new radical daughter looked pretty scary. I am sure my family was thrown in a whirlwind. Here I am one day wearing dark colors and being disrespectful and uncaring. Then all of a sudden I am hanging out with different friends, people they never met before. I am carrying and reading a Bible; I am even going to church during the week! Bible studies at different homes. My mom was beside herself, maybe scared and worried about my new radical change. She did not want any part of it, did not want me having Bible studies at our home, and just could not really pinpoint what was going on. This, of course, was because she did not understand. She does now! Things went on, and I continued to go to a local church enjoying my new friends. I graduated high school early and started working. Things were pretty good.

Now behind the doors, Dad was coming home two to three nights a week. He wasn't spending much time at the business. He had an open affair with a lady whose sons attended the same school as us. It was pretty heartbreaking, but I never told my mom. It lasted over seven years until someone told my mom they had pictures. Dad was going to be caught in the act and did not know how to get out of it.

My parents would soon divorce and things became difficult, mostly because Dad was not around as much as I would have liked. He lived for a short time with the lady he was having an affair with. My mom could not forgive him. She to this day has a difficult time being in the same room with him, but I do pray and believe it will happen soon. It has been a little difficult over the last thirty years to have family birthdays and functions as you may imagine! A lot of you may be able to relate. My dad, of course, has no problem, but my mom still has a lot of hurt. I know now mentally that he was abusive, but I sure wished at the time that she would forgive him, not just for me, but most of all, for herself, in order be able to move on and to cleanse her own hurt.

If you recall, I mentioned earlier that it took many years for me to have a relationship with my mom, mainly because I did not love myself, nor did I know how to forgive.

I thank God I am in a different place now with my God, family, and myself.

You know, growing up, we tend to want to blame others for whom we have become, what we have become, or we just take the easy way out and write people off. One lesson I learned through this process of learning forgiveness is that people are in our lives for a reason; our circumstances are a part of who we are and what we have become. Each of us, as individuals, have our own stuff to carry around, and many of us see things behind those closed doors that I can only imagine. But I have learned that these situations and individuals that cross our paths are sometimes a part of who we stand for. Of course, in my younger years, none of that crossed my mind. As you read on, and you read about the encounters I have had, you will wonder, "How in the heck is that going to help her later?" Hold that thought, and you will see.

As a child and young teen, I just wanted to play and be loved. That is what most kids want. We are born with a pure heart, one that requires tending to, one that asks for love and one that is already willing to love in return.

How many times did you as a child tell someone, "Hey, I'm just a kid"? We were feeling the pressures of childhood. Then there are going to be some of you that had to step into survivor mode more quickly than others. I am so sorry, and I pray that as you read this, it does not bring up harsh feelings of loss. Remember, our parents did not receive a manual to know how to raise us. Even if doctors have published many books, it is just not possible to know how each individual is going to develop. We are all different, and we all had different situations to overcome.

This is a cycle or chain that usually needs to be examined and sometimes broken, or the many family secrets can burden many generations. I wonder if forgiveness could be a unique antidote to breaking the chains.

Praise God for the many chains broken in my life!

5

First Love

I'm going to take you back a little before the divorce of my mom and dad in my early teens.

A part of me was still young and unsure of so many feelings. I still desired to have someone in my life. My family was breaking up right in front of my eyes.

> Cling tightly to your faith in Christ, and always keep your conscious clear. For some people have deliberately violated their consciences; and as a result have been shipwrecked. (1 Timothy 1:19)

For reasons I cannot explain, I missed my old friends; I felt strong enough to still hang out in places that I truly shouldn't be. It had been a short time that I had been walking with a new step—a grace that only God can give you. The drinking I had done in the past was a quick fix to my problems. This, I later found out, was a substance abuse. Thus began my drinking again. I did not continue going to church. I am not sure why; most likely it was shame. I can't really explain it.

I had a feeling of wanting to join in the fun! I can have one drink, maybe a few. One, of course, led to another, and before you know it, I was there again self-medicating.

Lord, the things I did while under the influence! I drank until I blacked out. I felt all the feelings from childhood surfacing. Unloved, unfair, unable, unlikely—every "un" word one could imagine.

I depended on my friends to bring me home safely. Sometimes they would literally drop me off at the front door, ring the bell, and leave. I was once again out of control. I still knew there was a God and sometimes would even call out to Him after I was sober enough to plan my next outing. I thank God for having me with people who actually took care of me. Every time I drank, I took myself to a next level, I vomited, I passed out, and sometimes I completely felt I was out of my mind!

One night I was at a friend's party. I was depressed and out of control again, drinking like a fish. I decided I was done—done again with life. I began to climb the silo they had on their ranch. I was nearly to the top when someone finally saw me.

I was stubborn and would not come down. They had to call their parents to try to talk me down. I was ready to jump. Their father was able to talk me down. I wept; there was no reason that I was alive. God had a bigger plan; of course, I just did not know. Not one person told my family; every one of my friends just knew I was pretty messed up in the head.

I went to sit in a truck. I cried, asked everyone to just leave me alone! After a little while, a young man who I will call First Love came to the window of the truck.

First Love was handsome. He had long, wavy beautiful hair; huge brown eyes; and a tenderness that I cannot explain. He wasn't one of the regulars around my circle of friends. I knew of him but did not really ever meet him before. We were in the 1970s in those days, and we wore big bell-bottom jeans, corduroys, white T-shirts, long jackets, and Derbies. The style of clothing was pretty fresh.

First Love was different, tender, and sincere. Sure, I had other short encounters with boys, but this one stood out for many reasons. He came to the window and asked if he could talk to me. I looked over deep into his eyes; they were soulful. I was mesmerized as I sat there wiping my tears from my face. Should I allow this person into my pain? He doesn't even know me. What would he think? It seemed like the world stopped as he looked at me through the window. I reached over and let him in the truck.

The moment he came into the truck, he held me. All I could do was cry. I am sure he could not understand a word I said. Once I started to pull myself together, I probably started to make a little more sense. He allowed me to spill my hurts onto his shoulder. We sat. He listened and he held me. I was amazed he did not want anything else from me. He was truly interested in what was hurting me; he truly cared about me. *Wow, that was unusual*, I thought. I still did not even like myself.

I fell head over heels in love with First Love. Oh, how I loved him! His family was everything to me. His mother loved and treated me as her own. He and I were together every day, every moment we could savor. We did not get intimate right away; he wasn't like that with me. We would just hang out and talk. The partying started to slow down too. First Love and I each got our driver's licenses about the same time. Before that, his mom used to pick me up every day and take me home every night. We were inseparable. First Love actually taught me how to drive a 1956 Chevy 3-speed truck. Those were the days. We enjoyed cars, and not just any cars—lowriders. We went to many car shows. I eventually bought a 1963 Chevy Super Sport. We were young and wanted to just run away and be married. We eventually decided that we would be intimate with each other. We decided not to use protection, and eventually I became pregnant. We were so very happy. I am pretty sure we both might have even planned it this way. Maybe now I could go and live with him.

My parents allowed us to be together; they did not worry any longer about me. They knew where I was and knew I was not in any trouble any longer. They surely did not think I would get pregnant.

They did get upset though. My mom and dad were worried about what people would think. They had a small business, and this would not fit their community image. I am sure people would have talked, but people talk about everything, right?

They began to pressure me into having an abortion. I could not believe it. Abortions were quite easy those days; I still could not believe it. Why not just let me be? My dad gave First Love an ultimatum: get a job and find our own place to live. Of course, this would be impossible; we were barely able to drive.

The worst came when they got a hold of First Love and his family and convinced First Love about how hard it was going to be to have a child. I succumbed to what they wanted, and I would regret this for a long time in my life. It was the most heartaching, painful experience I ever had. I would not ever feel the same. Life became dark and gray again for me. I did not like myself or anyone around me. I began drinking again, mostly to forget. It took me years of counseling and many, many hours of praying with people to be free of this guilt.

The darkness comes in and loves it when we hold on to things like this. It comes in and reminds you of how terrible you are and how no one in their right mind would ever love you, especially God. I finally was delivered from this pain a few years ago. Someone came to our church and discussed her painful abortion. I immediately felt that pain again. I was able to work with a lovely lady who walked me though the pain and reminded me I am a child of a mighty God, one that forgives and that loves me for who I am, not what I did. She taught me that this was my past and that God promises me I will see my child in heaven. You see, God doesn't forgive *some* of our sins; he forgives them *all*—each and every horrific one.

Well one day I felt bad and unworthy. I had gone out drinking with other friends and, of course, was making out with other boys. I could not face First Love, and I left him forever.

This would be a defining moment in my life.

6

Shame Does Not Have to Live Here No More

I wanted so badly to come back, to try again, but how could I? Writing this brings back many tears. It really hurts to be in a place that you feel will never go back to normal. I blew it, and how could anyone love me, especially First Love?

His family was truly the only healthy family structure I had. Losing that, I was a mess. The drinking began to take over my body and soul; people tried to reach out to me, but I was lost. I am not quite sure how it happened or why, but as the Word of God tells us, beware if you should fall. I continued with this lifestyle and ended up feeling overwhelmingly guilty. I was ashamed to come back to church and stayed away. My past began to haunt me again. I tried everything to take away the pains of my past. I eventually ran away and lived a life of party after party, many times not knowing where I was or how I even got there. My dad tried very hard to intervene, but I just would not listen. He even told me my mom wanted to hire a detective because they were so afraid of what I was doing. I think about the pain he must have felt to drive to my location and see me in that state of mind I was living less than a block away with some people I thought were friends. If you're a parent, can you even imagine driving away, leaving your daughter, and saying good-bye, not knowing what else to do? My poor parents.

With the alcohol came the sense of not having any value of my body, mind, or soul. One night I was drinking with four or five young men. I was about eighteen or nineteen at the time. We had been cruising around and drinking. Then we got to the apartment where we were going to be partying. I got out of the car and was overwhelmed; for some reason, I ran and I ended up in a dark apartment complex. One of the young men, whom I had just met that night, followed me. He saw how drunk I was. He found me and pinned me against a wall. He began to kiss me and tell me, "You know this is what you wanted. Now you are going to get it." I was unable to stop him. He began to pull down my pants and covered my mouth. I was right by the front door of an apartment. He raped me, pulled my pants up, and laughed and walked away, leaving me there crying. After he was done with me, he told me not to bother saying anything because no one would believe me. I remember running all the way to my friend, Monte's apartment. I remember running into his apartment, barely able to speak, and telling him everything that happened. He wanted to go after the person, but I would not let him go. I just needed him to help me wash off the nastiness of what had just occurred. I had sex with others casually, but this was different.

It was the first time sex made me feel disgusted. I was afraid to tell anyone, hearing the words "You know this is what you wanted" replay in my head over and over again. I just wanted to die.

Those words played in my head for over thirty years.

Monte worked steadily and had his own place. He was taller, Hispanic, and seemed a little more seasoned with life. He had a plan—more than any of us ever had. He was easy to talk to and had an opinion to give. He also had a girlfriend—a girl that he really liked. She was different than us, and that next morning she decided to come over to his place. Everyone that came over to drink was sprawled out in the living room with me in Monte's arms. He was consoling me. From the outside it looked different. She told him to never call her, and he was pretty upset. He called my parents and told them that I needed help. They came right over. I was a mess, but he did not tell them what really occurred, only that I needed to go home.

The next seconds, minutes, hours, and days of my life were dark and gray. In between my crying I recall myself looking out the window to the sky and calling out to God, "Why, Lord? Why me?" I had only told one person: Monte. I did not report it because the man who did this was right, who would believe me? I was drunk.

As one can imagine, things were pretty bad, I can't really remember how the blessing of meeting the wonderful people I met happened, although they were a crucial part of my life.

God sent two Christian families to me one day while I was out in the streets. I can only say it was a miracle. They loved me and carried me back to a place of dignity. I would later find out they were my prayer warriors. We began to meet for Bible studies regularly and walked the streets in our small town on fire for God. It was amazing. I was back home, living in my parents' house, and things started to come together. I was working again and clean and sober. Whew!

God had never left me; I walked away from Him.

My mom and dad were divorced. I did not get to see much of Dad, although we did get to see each other from time to time. My mom and I still had an estranged relationship. She was losing the house from the divorce. I still had a little resentment from the earlier things that went on, and don't know why I focused my blame on my poor mom and dad. As my family members were each going their own way, I was also going to have to find a place to live.

Monte and I began to see each other again, first as friends, and then we became more intimate. It was a crazy off-and-on relationship with Monte. We could never truly commit or completely break it off. My love for God grew stronger again; this time my mom was encouraging me to go to church!

God was an important part of who I was becoming and was present, and this of course made things a little different with Monte. He became second—no more sleeping around, no more drinking, no more drug use. I had no more time with him. He could not stand it.

7

Good Wife

Monte and I were now in this broken-off relationship for about six months. He couldn't stand that I was away from him, so he decided he would serve the Lord and marry me. He attended Bible studies with me and went to church with me. I was in heaven! Wow, this is amazing! He was a completely different person. Most adult Christians who have experienced new sobriety will tell you to make sure that whomever you are dating is sober for at least a year, that they have a good foundation in Christ, and that they are functional in their new faith. My friends told me to wait, but my body could not. One day, we got way too close. He cried telling me how much he loved me and that he needed me. Big red flag if someone needs you to survive! Lust got in the way, and I felt rushed into covering my sin. We met with our pastor at the time, who desperately tried to make us wait. We were going to run off to Reno if they did not marry us. So we were married. It was exciting to plan. My family was not there. I am not too sure why, but we did not want anyone to get in the way.

I knew the night of my wedding that I had made the biggest mistake ever! We went out to dinner with a couple of people who stood with us. Monte decided he would make a toast. He popped open champagne and tried to justify his drinking to celebrating a happy moment.

Far from it! Little by little I was unable to go to church, and I was drinking again, but only with him.

My new husband was gone most of the time. He wanted me to work to pay most of the expenses; he never wanted to help financially. He enjoyed his money. Sure, he had good things, but it was his money, not ours. I had a fairly good job at a new drugstore that opened in town.

Monte began to slowly control me; I was unable to wear certain clothes and could not wear makeup outside of the house. It was the closed-door thing again. Monte used to break me by telling me I would look like a whore even more than I already had been before.

I loved going to work and hated coming home. He watched what time I left and timed each trip to and from work. I could not even stop at the store because then he would question why I was late.

We had a small apartment, but it was home. My old friends were back in the picture, although they were a little more settled and married. Eventually they stopped coming over.

I had to go to the room whenever his friends would come over. I could not use the telephone; he used to feel it to see if it was warm when he got home. He did not allow me to go anywhere outside of work and home and began to abuse me mentally. At the time I did not know that this was abuse. He told me over and over again that I was lucky to even have him and that no one in their right mind would want to have me for their wife or girlfriend after what I allowed to happen to me. Remember, he was the only other person I had told about the rape.

I truly believed him and felt this is what life would be like until I died. Every now and then he would let me go to church; it was difficult. I was so afraid the friends from church would tell me, "We told you so," but they did not. The shame was overbearing, and eventually I stopped going. We did not have many intimate moments except every now and then when he would tell me he was sorry, we would drink together, and he would cuddle and love me for the night. Married, huh? What a thought at the time! I had no marriage.

I had gotten married to have someone to love and someone to love me not realizing or remembering that Christ could fill that void. My family at home was broken apart, and now I had my own broken family. I could not really go to my mom or dad; they were off on their own tangents plus they had to be pretty much fed up with me and my lifestyle from my past. I was not an easy teenager to be around.

I was now living a life like my parents. As I write this I wonder, could it have been a part of that learned behavior I mentioned before? I can't say, but as an adult I do believe that a lot of our examples are sketched into our brains.

I enjoyed working. When I went to work I was happy, and I worked hard to be promoted. I never was able to invite others over or go to work functions. When work was over, I prepared myself by washing my face before I left then got home to live another life behind closed doors.

Slowly I lost my identity; everything was about making Monte happy just so we could have a good evening. Maybe if I was lucky, we could sit and have a few drinks, and he would hold me.

The worst times were when he would leave and not return for two to three days. I was afraid to go anywhere and disrupt the routine. He could just pop in at any time or even sit in the car and watch me.

Things played over and over again in my head like I was in a movie!

We had moved to a little bigger place, and—you won't believe this one—I lived right next door to my mom. Even with her being so close, I had very little contact with her. She was always working, and I was too. Once I got home, I had to work hard at keeping things as sane as possible. Still, God knows what He is doing, and He listened to the many prayers being sent forth on my behalf.

One night, I had just finished preparing dinner for my husband. I was constantly trying so hard to do things right not to upset the man I was supposed to love until death do us part.

I placed a plate down on the table in front of Monte; he had a cold, stern face. It was as though he knew before I put the plate down that he was not going to approve. "You call that dinner?" he shouted, tossing the plate to the floor. I stood there looking down and not saying a word, trying not to provoke him anymore than I already had. I went to pick up the mess when he got up and said, "I'll be back. Clean up this mess." The door slammed behind him. There I was, sitting on the floor, cleaning the mess of what I had thought was dinner, crying and wondering, "Why me? What have I done to deserve this?"

Oh, yes, come on, Emily, you remember many things you had done. I truly thought I did deserve what was being done.

I cried so many times thinking of different ways I could make it up to him. *It was my fault anyway. I should know by now how he wanted his meals prepared. No wonder he was so angry. I'll show him I can be a good wife.* It was the beginning of a codependency that was so sick and controlling in itself.

All I wanted was to sleep now to prepare for tomorrow. The next day was my day off, and that meant lots of cleaning. I would have short windows of time that I could run next door for a quick visit or talk on the phone without him knowing. I had it all figured out. Of course, in the back of my mind, I felt guilty that I even made him so angry. How in the world could I make this man love me? Remember, you can never make anyone love you!

I lay in bed waiting for him to come home, watching the clock hands go by, sleeping in between hours, and waking to every car that I heard drive by.

Morning would arrive and no husband. *Well no wonder,* I thought, *you really got him mad this time. He'll be home soon, and this time I'll cook the way he wanted me to. I'll show him I can be a good wife.*

In between waiting for him I'd be praying that he was still alive and not in a car accident.

8

A Moment of Freedom

I had one good friend at the time: Veronica. I wasn't allowed to talk to her on the phone; remember, he used to come home and feel the phone to see if it was warm! When my husband was gone, I would try to call her just to see how she was and to have her make me laugh. She was always good for a joke.

"Hey, Emily, there is going to be a party tonight. Can't you try to come? We haven't seen you in *sooo* long."

"Oh, Veronica, things are so bad here at home. I don't think I could."

I explained to her what had been going on; she cried. She had no idea. I never wanted anyone to know how bad things were in my home.

"Emily, why didn't you ever talk to me? That's what a friend is for. You're a good wife," she assured me.

Then she told me something I couldn't believe: my husband was selling drugs. "No!" I thought it couldn't be true. How could I not know these things were going on in my home?

I heard the doorknob turn. "Veronica, I have to hang up; he's here." Quickly I ran to the front room so that he wouldn't suspect I was on the phone.

"Where have you been? I've been so worried," I said.

"I'm home, right? That's all that matters!" he shouted. Then he said he was going to bed and went upstairs. It had been two days since I last saw him. I sat alone and cried. It happened this way many times; I should have been used to it by now. The feeling of not being worthy of any other life would creep into my mind often.

9

Emily's Moment to Love at Last

One day, I'm not quite sure how it happened, but there I sat in a doctor's office waiting for the results of a pregnancy test. Monte and I had only slept together once during that month, and I was so afraid. Monte told me he could barely touch me because he said it made him sick. I looked up to see the doctor approaching me, and he could see the tears in my eyes. "Congratulations, Emily." That confirmed what I thought—a baby. Wow, I never would have even dreamed this could happen. In my teen years I had to have surgery on my ovaries. I was left with only half of one ovary. Doctors were not sure if I would have a hard time conceiving—another reason I was upset about the abortion.

Suddenly, joy filled me from head to toe. I had someone I could love and someone who would love me in return. I could now be a good mother.

As the days and weeks turned to months, I enjoyed every moment. Oh, how I loved the feeling of her kicking and rolling in my swollen belly! Thank God for my child within! The feeling of having someone to love that would love me in return was such a blessing. I thanked God every day. Since I was unable to leave the house, I had not been to church in a very long time. I tried to keep my faith alive with prayer.

> I urge you, first of all, to pray for all people. As you make your requests, plead for God's mercy upon them, and give thanks. (1 Timothy 2:1)

My personality began to change. I was no longer afraid anymore. My husband couldn't stand the fact that my family would come by every day to check on me. He wasn't able to abuse me mentally as much any longer. He was slowly losing control; what he would say did not matter as much as it did once. All I would think about was myself and my baby; that's all that mattered. I would be a good mother.

Well the moment finally came—labor pains. I had no idea what I was in for. My sister took me to the hospital while my mother and a few friends went ahead to meet us. My husband was at work. I told him not to worry because we could take care of everything. I really didn't want him around since this was my baby. Monte did not do well in hospitals anyway.

On October 14, 4:14 p.m., she was finally born—my baby. She was strong and healthy! Praise God! Her name would be Crystal Star. I didn't get to see her until she was four hours old due to being under sedation from my cesarean. All I knew was I had a girl and that she was healthy. Once I did see her I was in immediately in love! She had dark hair and eyes and beautiful olive-colored skin. I had never felt that kind of love before in my life. I finally had someone to love that would love me back, the kind of love I've always dreamed of—unconditional love.

When it was time to come home, my sister picked me up. What a joy when we finally got to go home! My family knew things were bad, but they stayed out of that part of my life.

The next few weeks were everything I thought they would be. Waking to breastfeed my baby was the most fulfilling experience I had ever known. There was no one in our little world besides her and me. Monte did not want to hold her too much; he said she was too small.

My husband still was never home. He actually came home one night and said he was sleeping with prostitutes and wanted to know how I felt about that; it didn't matter any longer. Sure, I would cry from time to time, but not as much as before.

I had someone to love who loved me back; I was a good mother.

10

A Defining Moment

Our home life was the same as it had always been. My husband did as he pleased, and I worked and came home to care for my daughter.

One day I was cleaning our bedroom—my bedroom, I should say, since I was the one who slept in it. I was going through the closet when I noticed a scrunched brown paper bag tossed behind the shoes. I reached for it while trembling, wondering if it could be what I didn't want it to be. I opened it with my hands shaking. I looked inside and stared in disbelief; it was a huge bag of marijuana. I continued to search the closet to find more surprises. A scale, baggies, and rolls of twenty-dollar bills wrapped with rubber bands. I couldn't believe it. It was true. He is selling drugs.

Stopping for a moment to think, I put everything back. *I'll pretend I never found anything,* I thought, shaking inside. *But wait, what about the baby? This would not be good for her or me.*

Or this could be my way out of this so-called marriage. I trembled as I grabbed the bag again and went downstairs to get Crystal. I decided to take her to my mother's apartment. God placed her next door for a reason! I knocked on the door with Crystal in my arms. My mom was home. I told her of my discovery. My mom was in shock as well; I asked her to keep Crystal with her while I did what I thought had to be done. She agreed. I also advised her to call the police immediately if she heard me knock on the wall. She took Crystal in her arms, and I turned and walked back to my apartment. Crystal cried out for me: "Mommy!"

My heart began to pump harder, knowing the decision I had made could be dangerous. Monte had a thing about his stuff: no one touched it, not even me. I got the bag and went into the bathroom. I pulled out the burnt-rope smelling contents and held it over the toilet, letting it fall little by little until the bag was empty. I reached for the handle and pushed it down, watching till it was all gone. There was no turning back now. I left all the money on the bed, and I threw the scale out in the back dumpster and then went back in the apartment. I called my best friend, Veronica, and she said, "I told you." She told me to look in the freezer under some wrapped meat, and I would find some foil-wrapped packages as well. Her husband had come over, and my husband had bragged to him about what he was doing and how stupid I was. I found the small bundles and flushed the contents as well.

Then came the hard part. I was shaking in my shoes. Replaying what to say and where and how I could escape—it was crazy. Should I call the police? Oh, Lord I did not know what I was doing, but the clock kept ticking, and the time was coming very soon for Monte to walk into that door. He had a routine, and this was a weekday. This meant home by 4:00 p.m., walk in, go upstairs, change, and go for a run. There I sat, waiting for him to walk in through the door. All I could hear was the loud ticking from the clock as I was waiting for him to come home. I'm not sure what was louder, the ticking from the clock or the pounding of my heart.

I heard the door; he was home. Monte went straight upstairs as he always did, not even noticing I was in the front room. He was up there for a few minutes when I heard, "Emily, where's my shit?" He stormed downstairs.

"I flushed it down the toilet," I answered, my voice shaking.

"You. Stupid. Bitch! Do you know how much money that was?" He came toward me, and I ran toward the door. He grabbed me and pinned me by the throat to the wall. I put up my hand and said, "Look [this would be the first time I ever answered him back], you have no right putting my baby and me in this kind of danger. I have taken enough. Here is your option, Monte. Both you and I go to counseling, or you leave. If you go, there is no coming back, that's a promise." He chose the door, as I knew he would, and I kept my promise. He tried to come back home after two weeks, but I would not let him. I had to get a restraining order because he would threaten to wait for me after work with a gun. I had to be walked out to my car for about six months. I was finely free though, thank God!

This is when the story seems to end happily, and you would think I would end up walking with the Lord again, praising God for my freedom. I feel bad telling you, but I did not. I was so lost and yet felt free. Instead of finding ways to get back with God, I chose to drink and live the crazy life of partying and going out and about. I wasn't strong or standing firm in the Word of God, nor did I have any contact with a family of believers for strength.

The thing that was different through all of it was that after those crazy nights I would cry and ask God to help me stop.

Wonderful things happen with time. Today Monte and I are now able to be in the same room together. We are respectful to each other, and we both love our daughter with all of our hearts.

In my mind I believe Monte had many things going on within his own young life or within himself and his own identity. There were many young adults doing drugs and getting caught up in selling them. Money was something any young teen living on his own would be attracted to. I do not believe he meant to be so strong and hurtful. He was a very caring man before we got together, but we were very young. We had an unhealthy relationship that unfortunately took a turn for the worse.

The best thing ever is that we have a beautiful daughter. She is strong and very courageous.

11

Second Chance at Love

I just have to take a moment to process all that I have told you. I am amazed at how, through it all, we still have a fight in us, a fire-eating strength that I am unable to describe. You see, each of us has one—that fight. God instills us with love and the Holy Spirit to fight our battles. I just didn't know how powerful I could be at times.

Having a full-time job is part of why I got strong enough to leave. I got a little stronger and began to finally share what was going on. Most of us who are in a mentally or physically abusive situation try not to reveal what goes on behind our doors. It is part of our survival mode, but that will begin to eat us alive, and the dangerous circumstances that can develop from this type of abuse can kill us from within. We eventually lose who we are and become who our partner wants us to be.

In the midst of all that was beginning to aspire, I was starting to befriend a new employee named Murle. Murle was coming from a nearby city and was also looking to begin a new chapter in his life. He was different from the others; having someone new that would listen was important to me.

Murle used to talk to me at lunchtime and bring me roses, beautiful cards, letters, and notes—anything and everything to brighten my day.

I am sure any one of you would want to lift up my spirits. Just listening to my stories about home would take you to a place of sorrow.

My work ethic was very good; I climbed my way up to photo manager and then bookkeeper, trusted with thousands of dollars! I was invited to after-work functions and would of course join. My social drinking was under control. I had an image that was important to me. Murle and I became closer and closer. He was a very good listener and handsome. We eventually decided to be in a committed relationship. We loved each other.

He had a story as well, and I immediately began to try to fix his little world. Crystal enjoyed us being together; she called him Daddy Murle.

Monte, as one can imagine, was extremely upset. There were a few times that he followed us, and Murle had to get out of the car and talk to him, trying to be logical and not have a yelling match.

We ended up moving in together. Murle never knew about my walk with the Lord. Jesus was pushed aside a little while I entertained my new life. What was I thinking? Oh, I forgot to mention Murle was seven years younger than me.

Things were good for a while. I really had no time to drink like I was before because of my responsible life. Plus, I had to try and create this perfect life for everyone to witness, especially because many of Murle's friends and relatives warned me to be careful with him—he had a past of being irresponsible. I, of course, wanted to prove them wrong, wanted to paint a pretty family—one that no one could take apart, one that looked good from the outside of the door.

Murle was good to me, and he loved Crystal as a daughter. I later found out he had a son at the young age of fifteen. We worked together to begin paying child support to help him get his license back and to have visits. Murle had never had the things I worked hard to achieve: credit cards, health insurance, and a car. He eventually began to ask for things, not just little things. Expensive things like customized golf clubs and money for outings with his cousins. He was trying to fit in places that he had not been able to go prior to meeting me because of not having money. Eventually, he had, with my permission, racked up all of my credit cards. We were over $10,000.00 in debt. He had no car, and I was not in a position to buy him one. I was getting a little frustrated. Wouldn't you?

One day, about six months or so later, I started to feel a little sick. I wasn't sure what it was. I went to the doctors and wow!

Yup, I was pregnant. I was going to have another beautiful angel. My dad had remarried by then, and my new mom was included in our joy. She was the first one I called because she did not judge me; she loved Dad, her children, and their families unconditionally. She was one of the most caring and giving souls I knew. God truly blessed us by allowing us to be in her world. She later went to be with the Lord. We all miss her terribly, but knowing we will see her again gives us some comfort.

Murle was happy and could not believe it. Neither could I since I did not think I was going to have any more children. So our new life began. I continued to be the responsible one—I had to be. Murle and I worked different shifts in order to share the car and save on day care for Crystal.

I am not quite sure how we get that feeling of "someone is being unfaithful," but we do. We get a little tug in the stomach and a question in our head. Then we begin to question everything until we are obsessed. Finding out was my goal, and I did. Murle was having an affair with a new girl at work. She was cute, young, and did not care about me. Others told her it was not right, but they both carried on. One day I got her address and went there because Murle left early that day. Sure enough, there was my car in the driveway. I pounded on the door and told him to get out! I probably used some really bad words. He came out trying to say it wasn't what I thought. He did his little smooching to make up, and I forgave him, but with caution. Then I ended up getting some pains and found out I had contracted an STD!

"Really, are you kidding me?" I questioned him. I had believed him that he had not gotten intimate with her. Now we had to take medication and tell her to take some too. Thank God it was not one of the really dangerous STDs, but just the thought of it made me sick. She eventually quit her job. Murle continued to have these little flings with new cashiers. One time I caught him right in my bookkeeper's office. I was going in one door, and he was running out the other! Things were not easy; he continued to want more material things. He was not up to par as his cousins were; they had good jobs, good cars, and money to do whatever they wanted. Murle did not; he had his son and us to help support.

I was pregnant then and just figured I would have to adjust. Things were never the same for us. There never was a true trust or forgiveness. Eventually we moved to a small house his parents owned to try to save money and get ready for my beautiful baby. Murle tried to be as responsible as possible, but he was young, and it was just difficult for him.

On February 27, I went into labor. It was a long two days, but on February 29 at 5:17 a.m., she arrived. Buttercup was what Murle called her. She was and still is beautiful. My new angel's name is Sapphire.

12

Drugs Take Over

Things were what I expected; I stayed home and loved my daughters. Crystal and Sapphire are five years apart. Crystal helped take care of her baby sister in many helpful ways. Now I had two beautiful girls that God is entrusting to me!

That is a lot of responsibility, Lord! But oh so worth it; they are my world, and I praise Him for them every day.

Murle and I had a lot of disagreements. He was now becoming more and more distant from the use of drugs and alcohol. I watched as he descended into a cycle so well-known to me.

There were many yelling matches, throwing of pots and pans, and plain crazy fighting.

With Murle's drug use, there were other personalities, some with rage.

On one occasion I was sitting on the porch, and a car drove up. A couple of guys came out of the car stating that Murle owed them over $1,000.00. I told them I knew nothing about it, we had no money, and that if they wanted, they could take anything that belonged to him. This should have been enough for me. Some of Murle's friends would try to talk to me and get me to leave him, but it was difficult. I had the girls, and I felt a little trapped. One day, I was home with the girls when Murle came home early from work. He came in through the door; his eyes were bloodshot as though he had been up for days. He went straight to the room and asked me for money. He grabbed my purse and shook everything out of it. The girls were out on the front porch. He became very agitated with me not having any money and started looking in drawers, throwing things, and yelling at the same time for me to find money! I ran after him in the front room. He went into the kitchen and went to open a top cabinet above the refrigerator. There were pots and pans on top, and as he opened the cupboard, the pans hit me in the head. My daughter told me I fell to the floor and blacked out. He ran out and sped off in a car. The girls were in the living room, and they ran to help their mommy. I came to and told the girls to get whatever they could into the car quickly, and we left. We ended up at my sister's house, each of us shaken by what had just occurred.

In the midst of all the chaos, I had started talking to one of Murle's friends. He used to come over from time to time with one of our best friends. His name was David. He was funny and loved sitting with me and talking. He was newly divorced and had a daughter the same age as Crystal. I became strong again, and my fire-eating personality began to burn inside. I put my big-girl pants on, got on my feet, and moved out.

I had a small one-bedroom apartment, but it was mine and my girls'. I fell head over heels in love with David. We had such good times together; slowly our times were focused more at being together when the girls were with my sister and her husband or when they had visits with their fathers. David and I began to spend more and more time drinking together. I was becoming what some refer to as a functional alcoholic drunk: stupid on the weekends and back to reality on the weekdays. David introduced me to country music; we enjoyed going out dancing together. It was a completely new world to me. I even learned how to dance the fourteen-step.

Things began to get a little unsettling between us because David began to get really jealous. My new job required me to dress nice. I had to start going to his place at lunchtime to check in. Slowly but surely, the cycle of being controlled started again. We never moved in together, but it was very dysfunctional.

My sister and brother-in-law were such lifesavers; they cared for my daughters many weekends to help me get things in order.

It amazes me how we think no one knows, but there are big eyes watching us. God knows all!

One night during one of our fun weekends, David began talking about how maybe we should take a break. He thought it would be best because he could tell I was starting to feel a little stressed with our relationship. I pleaded with him, "Please, no. I will do whatever you need."

I was a mess that Sunday after he left. Deep inside it just did not make sense. *We had been doing great together,* I thought. I had even gotten a loan and bought him a Harley! What else could be going on? I decided to go to his home. I knocked, but he did not answer the door. I began calling and calling, leaving message after message.

One night I watched his home. Yes, I stalked him. I got that sick feeling I mentioned before, that instinct that something was going on. I had my friend drive the car, and we followed him, and he went to a little trailer park. I watched as he went in and kissed someone at the door! What the heck? I was sick to my stomach. I had my friend wait in the car, and I knocked on the door. The other woman answered the door and seemed so apologetic. "Why didn't you tell her the truth, David?" she asked. *What truth?* I thought. David came out and said, "It is over." I stood there crying at the steps and pleading with him to please not leave me. My friend got me to get back into the car and took me home. I went into my room, lay on my bed, and wept. This was my next experience of wanting to die. My depression was bad; I would not get up nor go to work. I remember one day Crystal came to me and said, "Mommy, please, I know you're sad. Please get up." It was heartwrenching. How did I get myself into these situations? All this happened in a little over six months. One thing I learned about codependency is one can never make someone love another; he or she loves on his or her own. Love is a gift, and it should be shared equally. But it was like trying to keep my dad home, trying hard to be good, or trying to be a good wife all in order to have things in place. I mostly wanted someone to love me.

It took me about a week to get myself together. Emotionally, it was not a good place to be. But I did get up and go to work. I made a vow: no more men! I sailed along, focusing on my girls and saving money for better things for us. I had a wonderful day care provider and family who believed in me. They provided love and counseled me back to reality.

13

My Way Back Home

The girls and I were happy again. There were many struggles, but we were doing fairly well. One day I got a speeding ticket and had to go to traffic school to clear the ticket.

One of my dear friends from the store I worked at when I met Murle was teaching the class.

That is how God works. I needed to settle down a little in order to listen carefully.

Well, you can only imagine; once my friend started to talk to me about what God was doing in her life, I knew I was in safe company. She and her husband invited me to church, and, yes, the girls and I went. It was awesome. The people were so kind, and I loved it. The girls were about three and eight, and I decided to dedicate them with a special service at the church. Life was good.

Finally, God sent someone to share Christ's love and forgiveness. I was able to identify myself with the church as family. I got sober and was enjoying life again. One day, one of the band members asked me for a date. His name was Jonah. I couldn't believe it. Me? Are you kidding me?

About this same time Murle and I had started to talk again. He was out of jail and wanted to start helping me again. He asked us to live in his mother's home so I could save money. He was unable to pay child support, and he felt really bad. I spoke to his mother, and she wanted the same. We at least were friends; he just wanted badly to be a part of the girls' lives again. He seemed sincere enough, and he was sober. I definitely needed to save money. He had been in jail for almost a year and felt a deep remorse for all the pain he had caused us in the past.

Jonah and I began to see each other often over the next few months. I was mesmerized at how he never kissed me or got too close; this was his protection mode. He had a story too and was trying hard to not get into any more trouble. We both knew getting too intimate would only get us in trouble. Both our kids enjoyed seeing us together, and they actually planned our engagement. He was good for me at the time—safe.

I decided to start going back to school. Just one class, but it was a start. I was tired of trying to make enough money to take care of the girls by myself. Murle was doing well, and our living situation was good. He had also been staying in a separate room at his mother's home.

One day when I was getting ready to go to church, Murle took Sapphire and locked himself in the house. He had slipped and was under influence. He said he did not like me seeing anybody else. I looked for help and finally had to call the sheriff. The deputies had to surround the house before Murle finally came out. He had to go back to jail. His mother was upset I called the sheriff and told us we had to leave. I packed our belongings and once again moved. It all happened within a day. I stayed with my sister for a short time. I felt so depressed and betrayed.

The odd thing was Jonah did not even call me or check on me; he just disappeared.

I am sure now, as I think of it, he had to; I probably had a huge red flag over my head.

Once again I was starting all over, this time in a different city. I was driving forty-five minutes to work at four in the morning. It was just crazy. I did not drink though. I did pretty well considering everything. I tried some secular meetings, but I just could not get into saying, "My name is Emily, and I am an alcoholic." Yeah, I knew I could be one, but what I knew for sure was that God forgave me, and I did not have to label myself over and over again.

Slowly I got myself to a place in the same city I was now working in—our own new place. The girls had to move around a lot during all these transitions. Remember I told you how difficult that was for me? Now I was doing the same thing to them. I felt terrible, but we had to move. I had a decent job and could not keep driving so much and taking the girls to day care so early in the morning. We eventually got settled in; the girls were doing well in school, and all seemed to be just right again. Yet I was no longer going to church.

14

Searching

Everything had happened in a little over five years since my divorce in 1985. So much, right? I had been single now for what I thought was a while. One day, one of my coworkers decided to introduce me to someone—a blind date. He did not show up the first time or the second time. Finally, on the third time, I met him. His name was Greg.

Greg's mother met me and told me, "You don't want to be around him, he is not your type." I did not listen. I guess now it was a challenge.

I was still emotionally sick, trying to see if I could make someone interested in me. I did not like *not* having a man in my life, although just allowing any man to fill that void is not okay.

I still did not completely know how much I was worth.

Greg was tall and looked like a big Native American Indian chief. He had a good job and was funny. There was something peculiar about him, but I did not get it. About this time I was still taking one class at a time. I was beginning to become a little more confident about my education. Greg was coming around, but not too much. It was a little bizarre because he would say he was coming over, but then wouldn't. I wouldn't hear from him for a while, and then he would call after a few days saying he wasn't feeling well. We had not become intimate yet, but when he would come by, he would bring flowers. Seemed okay, I guess. Was he respecting me? That would be new for me. One day, we finally had time alone together for a weekend. We had some drinks and had a fun time. The challenge was still there: for some reason, he was just unpredictable. Later I would find out it was because he was into heavy drugs. This was why he was in and out. I don't know why or how I could allow it, but he moved in. The girls did not like it because they were very protective after what happened with David. I don't blame them at all. I assured them it would be okay. Sometimes it was, but eventually, most of the time it wasn't. I became very aware of his drug use. His mood swings were extreme. His highs were when we could get money to go out to eat and buy clothes or whatever the girls wanted. These lasted three days. When the crashes came, they came hard. We let him sleep. We had to keep quiet because he would become agitated, yell, and make us miserable. The girls and I slept together in their room. I had to lock his door a lot so they would not see him. Sapphire confided in me recently she had found his drugs.

One day he said we were going to get a new apartment, a nice one so that the girls could have their own room and bathroom. We were excited; the apartments were big and very nice. I had just finished my associates' degree in paralegal studies. Can you believe it? And I got straight As.

We packed and started moving. Greg got us moved but did not join us. I was confused he wasn't coming home. He showed up a couple of days later. "What is going on?" I asked him. He told me he had another girlfriend and was going to be living with her.

"Are you kidding me? I can't afford this place, you know that," I said.

He left. I was at a loss. I was in shock. He had encouraged me to go to school and had been that person who, when he could, supported my education. I think that he was trying to help me get on my feet so that I would leave him. He knew I should not be with him.

I was a little afraid, a little relieved, and a little hurt. The next couple of days were crazy and blurry. I had found a new job managing a store about an hour away. Crazy thing is one of the managers happened to be one of the managers from the store I worked at with Murle. Tom was his name; I trusted Tom and told him my woes and worries. He was sorry for my pain and told me he loved me, that he always had loved me. He used to worry about me when I was with Murle. Tom was a kind man; he had a daughter, had been through a painful divorce, and, best of all, he had a good listening ear.

He really was not my type. Really, did I even have a type?

We started to become a couple. I had to find a new job and did so rather quickly since we could not work in the same store if we were in a relationship. I had a good work history, so it was not long before I found a new job.

My drinking increased on my days off, and I drank heavily at night. Tom used to bring me a 40 oz. at night to help me sleep. Things got rushed, and he asked me to move in with him. I did not have enough money to pay my rent. Here I was again moving in with someone I thought I knew. We got engaged within a month! I was so messed up he did not even know how bad it was. How could I love him? I hated myself. Finally, one day, I could not stand myself. I called my family and told them I needed out of the situation I got myself into and that my drinking was out of control again. I remembered that my employment had one of those telephone numbers on a card that you can call for confidential assistance. I called, and they helped me through my mess. They got me into a rehabilitation center, and I was able to stay there for a month. During this time I was able to break all my shame and peel all of my layers with the help of professionals. It was exactly what I needed. I even got some time with my mom by myself to talk to her about my earlier grudges.

My poor babies had to split their time between my sister and their day care provider. I can only imagine how difficult that it was for them. They had no father, and now their mommy was gone too. The girls were able to see me for a brief visit on one weekend. It was heartwrenching, but I told them Mommy had to get better. The girls drove away feeling sad, overwhelmed, and alone. The girls had to go to school with this heavy burden.

Our chaos does need to be recognized. There are many kids walking around like zombies, coming from things like the story I am sharing. Hurt, alone, unsure, afraid, and shamed.

Please remember this as you work through your things.

If you are working with children or young teenagers, smile and look past their faces; it will make a difference.

Getting back to my story, it was agreed that I was not well enough to be in a relationship, and the staff doctors helped me to break it off with Tom. He took it well, but I felt bad. He deserved to know that I was not in love with him and that I needed to be alone to work on myself. Once again my sister and brother-in-law were there to help me get on my feet. I found a new job and started to pull my life back together.

I finally found a church to attend, and with the help of the pastor, I was able to begin my studies towards my BA in addiction studies at Bethany College in Scotts Valley. I was able to get my own apartment near my family. My girls had been through so much by now, and yet they saw me get up again, this time to continue with school. They used to have to come with me to class and sit in the back. Gas was getting expensive for the more–than-an-hour's drive. My classes were Friday night and all day on Saturday. One day my professor asked me if I would like to sleep on campus; he said I could stay in the synagogue with the girls. We brought our sleeping bags the next week and stayed on campus. My daughters were my inspiration. Through the first two years we did this every weekend. My grades were good, I was clean and sober, and we had our own place. My life was getting back on track. I loved my new church family, and they truly cared about me.

God provided me a new career within the local high school. I loved the new challenge.

I am not sure how it all happened, but all of a sudden Greg called and wanted to talk. I should have said no, but I wanted to see what he had to say. He was sorry for everything and had been clean and sober for six months, he said. Drinking and drugs were all he was about, but my sick mind thought he changed. He came to Bible studies with me and accepted Jesus as his savior; the girls hated having him back in our lives. I got caught up in having someone in my life again. We eloped to Monterey and got married. I don't know what I was thinking; within a few weeks he began to drink again and use drugs. He went crazy, and I had to call the police.

Me and my girls packed our things and left till he was gone. Finally free! I was able to obtain a divorce quickly. I still had my employment, thank God.

The craziness with Greg was very dysfunctional and codependent. Just thinking about my poor girls and what they had to witness makes still makes me sick. I have learned to forgive myself and have asked for forgiveness from my daughters. They tell me that they are stronger because they have watched me throughout all the chaos pick myself up and continue moving forward.

Believe it or not, now as I look back through it all, I can now see how God had his hand in all of it. This would all be a part of my story.

I had stopped going to church again probably because I was slowly beginning to drink again. I am still unable to pinpoint it. Could it have been that moment of freedom again? Also, I was not firmly grounded in God's word. God's word provides us with the rock we need to stand on. Everything else can be broken, but His word does not fail.

15

Purpose in Life

I graduated with a 3.75 GPA, of which I was proud of. For the last ten years I had been in and out of chaos, yet still I was able to complete school. God had instilled a drive in me that I cannot even to this day explain. Once I graduated, I was approached to try teaching. I never thought I would be smart enough to be a teacher. The director of special education had complete faith in me and asked me to try. I am so happy that she believed in me; this was the beginning of my career and my clear purpose in life: a life dedicated to working with students with special needs. God's wonderful children whom he entrusted with me! Everything seemed to be going wonderfully. I had not been faithful with serving God at this time; I believe it had already been about four years since I had last been to church. I was drinking responsibly, sometimes too much on the weekends. The hangovers were terrible. I was getting tired of it all.

For some reason, I really cannot explain why, I got physically lonely again. Why would I have the need to go out and look for love in all the wrong places after being alone for many years? I still had not dealt completely with the many things that had occurred throughout my life.

The failures at marriage made me feel bad, and I did not go to church.

I did remember I could pray and asked for forgiveness many times, but I continued to fall almost weekly. This cycle would continue. I always had the love of Christ in my heart and cried out to him quite frequently, but I was not serving him. I felt shipwrecked.

> [18] Timothy, my son, I am giving you this command in keeping with the prophecies once made about you, so that by recalling them you may fight the battle well, [19] holding on to faith and a good conscience, which some have rejected and so have suffered shipwreck with regard to the faith. (1 Timothy 1:18–19)

I always felt so alone. The physical desire to have someone in my life was strong.

I raised my girls as best as I could. By now my girls were all grown up and gone, and all my friends were married. It was just heartbreaking for me to be on my own. Maybe the thoughts in my head were right; I couldn't be good enough for any man to share my life with. Maybe this was my punishment for doing all the terrible things I had done.

I had been gone from the old town where my mom and dad had moved us. I would have panic attacks if I ever had to drive through it even on the freeway. I would not get gas even if I needed it. I had such a fear and was always ashamed to stop in that town, afraid to see anyone I had known from my past, especially the person who raped me. I was sure he told everyone and that they would mock me. If I stayed away, I could block it out of my mind. I was drinking and living the high life; I wonder how I am even still alive. Perhaps this could only be the grace of God. I began to have little value for my body again and started to date more and more. I wish I would have just gone back to church and again found that fire-eating desire for courage.

I am wondering along with you, "What the heck is wrong with you, Emily?"

16

Last Love

I met Last Love at a small blues club in Sunnyvale. He and I were both on separate blind dates, both not going well. We exchanged numbers at the bar and left it at that. A few months later—and a few men later—I found his card and decided to call him. I had my wonderful career of teaching, blessed with my beautiful special-needs kids, and I always thanked God for it!

Last Love was my age; he was a big biker and rough around the edges. He had this quirky personality and loved to talk. Boy, did he like to talk. He had a good job and seemed to be responsible. He was looking for a home in the town I grew up in (that's right, the town I feared to drive through). He had a motorcycle that I really enjoyed. We used to go on long bike rides. He was Caucasian, not Mexican, unlike all the other men in my past. He did drink though; he was a functional drinker.

He told me he loved my free spirit and the fact that I danced alone and seemed to love life. Last Love and I began to see each other weekly, and then he asked me if I would like to live with him. Knowing it was against my personal religious beliefs, I still did. As time went on, I made a home out of the house he purchased, and we shared expenses. My family figured I knew what I was doing and gave me their blessings. It was our home, and it was a beautiful house. My girls visited from time to time, but they had their own little families. I had been blessed with grandchildren by this time.

Last Love's love was different for me; he had lost his mother a year earlier, had a really good job, and had it all together, except sometimes on the weekends when he began to drink. He drank frequently to black out. We slept in separate rooms, part of the agreement of moving in. Our relationship was not based on sex; we just had an intense friendship. We talked and laughed so much. We went many places. Last Love just had so many pains.

I was commuting to work but soon had the opportunity of teaching at the very high school I graduated from! Within a year Last Love's drinking began to get worse, and he began to yell at me. His verbal abuse got worse over the next few months. His drinking binges were awful and lasted all weekend. Then the apologies would come, and I would forgive him and just try to love him better. I remember once crying and asking him to go to church with me. He used to hold me so tight and tell me he was so sorry. I needed normal again. I loved him so much; what was going on? I know he loved me; he told me over and over again. Most Monday mornings he would call me when he got to work simply to wake me up, but mostly to ensure me we were okay and for me not to worry. I did not want to leave, but he knew I was sad.

My depression was slowly taking a hold of me. We drank together, sometimes way too much. Eventually, I dreaded Friday evenings because he would think he deserved a beer or two after the long week he had. The sound of a can opening would give me anxiety. If any of you live with an alcoholic or live in an alcoholic home, you know what I'm talking about.

Last Love had racing thoughts that people were out to get him; it was hard for him to trust people. At last, I was called so many names and told to leave so many times. All I could do was cry. I used to go outside and sit on the porch to have peace and to think of a way out. I prayed for God to take me out!

One day, out of nowhere, I received a letter. You are not going to believe this. The letter was from First Love! He was thinking of me and really wanted to talk. The letter had his phone number. He had gotten my address from his mother, whom I had sent Christmas cards to over the years. The letter amazed me because we had not spoken in more than thirty years.

I waited till Last Love was asleep and called First Love. Oh, the joy we both had hearing each other's voices. We talked about everything. He had been thinking of me and wondered how I was. I mostly wanted to apologize for all the heartache I had caused him and that I wished I had not taken the route I did back then, but that in it all I had always still loved him.

He told me my young painful years had caused him a lot of heartache, car accidents, and moving to deal with the pain—a lot of pain. I felt really bad.

When we are sick in our addictions, we do not know the impact we make on other people's lives. First Love and I cried about the abortion and forgave each other. He told me he still had a hard time with that as well. Of course he would; it is understandable to have a hard time with something like that. It was a blessing to have my dear friend from the past to talk to again. He gave me inner strength again; he was the answer to my prayer in a sense, someone to help me realize enough is enough and it is okay to leave. At my age now, I was just tired of having to do this all over again. Was I going to ever figure things out? Was I ever going to have a normal relationship?

Remember that life of being someone different behind closed doors? Well now I was doing that once again. This chain needed to be broken! First Love and I continued to talk. Over the next few days I found my first Bible back from the man at the desk in my dad's store. Can you believe it? I still had it! So many memories were being uncovered. My Bible was filled with underlined and highlighted scripture from the past that was now relevant for my present.

That was a good day. Transformation was beginning.

First Love told me in one conversation that he had been a youth pastor for years and that he had fallen from the church as well. I exclaimed, "What? Are you kidding me? This was not by chance that we are talking again. You will get your life right with God."

"I know I am," he replied. And he did.

Have any of you heard that saying that God will make good out of every situation—every single one? I am living testimony to that as I share these words. You see, First Love needed my forgiveness, and I needed his. We both had fallen from serving a wonderful God, and who in a million years would have thought that God would use First Love to help me get out of Last Love's house?

I know God heard my cry. On March 19, 2011, Last Love got drunk. He was angry because I took too long with my eight-month-pregnant daughter, and he just figured in his mind that I did not want to be with him. He called and wanted me to go to Jack in the Box when I got home, and I said no and that I would make him something to eat or get him something closer to home. He did not like that at all.

When I got home he started to yell at me and called me names—not in the usual way but in a very, very threatening way. I said, "That's it. I am leaving." He followed me into my room as I packed and said, "Fine, go ahead and go. You think you can do better out there?"

"Yes," I said. He grabbed my bag realizing I really was leaving and said it was his bag. He threw all the contents on the bed then hit me with the bag. I ran, got my phone, and told him I was going to call the police. I ran into the bathroom, shaking as I called 911. I was crying in fear; I could hear him yelling from the living room. I needed help getting out of the house because the front door was at the other end of the house. The 911 operator got all of our information and asked about weapons.

"He doesn't need anything; he is 6'2" and very strong," was my answer. As I cried I tried to listen with my ear to the door. The 911 operator kept me on the phone. It was quiet for a second, and then the banging on the door startled me, and I began screaming! "Please hurry, I need help. He has never gotten this angry!" I could barely hear the sirens coming around the block, but it did not seem fast enough. He eventually banged the door open, wrestled with me, hit me with my brush, and took my phone and flushed it in the toilet in his room. When he went to his room, I ran for my life to the garage, pushed the garage door opener, and as the door started to open, I had just enough room to squeeze through I ran out to the street. The police were there surrounding the house—our home. They grabbed me quickly. I had no shoes, it was raining, and all the neighbors were now outside. The officers were so kind. They had me in a locked car and tried to begin their interrogation of how to get Last Love out of the house. It was like being in a movie—guns drawn and the officers waiting.

Finally, after what seemed like forever, I heard over the radio that he was going to open the garage door. He did but decided he would not come out. Again they drew their weapons and proceeded into our home through the inside of the garage. All I know of what happened next is that according the police report he would not get up from the couch; he actually opened another beer and told them they would have to carry him out. They grabbed him, took him down, and cuffed him. As he came out, I was still crying. The look on his face was one I had never seen on any man. His eyes were red; his face was stern and very scary. It was even worse than Murle's eyes that day many years ago.

I realized at that moment our relationship was now over. It was over, and there was no turning back. Too many people could now see the pain and heartache—the pain that was behind those doors.

The officer that stayed with me was patient; he did not demean me in any way, and he asked if I needed help, a counselor—anyone. I was pretty shaken up. "I just needed some time to think," I told him. I was so broken and hurt. How could someone that told me over and over again how much they loved me and whom I loved so very much—more than myself—hurt me this way? I sat alone for a minute and then called a coworker, who in turn called a parent of one of my students because she would be closer to my home to come and help. She came right over, and I just sat there and cried, still in shock. All I wanted was wine and cigarettes. I could not leave my home. My friend stayed till she knew I was feeling better and encouraged me to call my daughter. I called my oldest daughter. All I said was, "Crystal, I think I want to move." She said okay and came right over; she never asked what happened or why. When she arrived, I packed a few things, and as we drove back to her house, I told her what had occurred.

I wish I had loved God as much as I loved Last Love. Look how much He loved me; He got me out alive.

My oldest daughter and her husband opened their home to me. They got all my things out of the other house in twenty-four hours because that is all the time the police were going to be able to hold Last Love. No one asked me any questions. They were just there to help. It was difficult to be in the house and to see it empty as I left. I realized all the love I had brought into that home.

Over the next few weeks there was a lot of pain and tears and grief.

Instead of going to God—you know already—I began to drink in order to forget, my way of self-medicating.

One night my daughter told me that she was embarrassed of me when I drank and that she did not want her children around me in that state of mind. Her words hurt me so much. I thought a lot about that and cried to God for healing. I asked Him once again for help. A church family, Lord, in order to get my life back on track. I was done—fed up and done! Time for the fire-eater to come out! I know You're still in me!

That next Sunday God lead me to a local church and gave me courage to walk through its doors. I cried all through the service and recommitted my life to Christ.

Thank you, Jesus. Hallelujah! My faith was renewed, and God began to become alive in my heart.

17

Life as I Knew It Stopped

Things were going really well; I had a new church family, my daughters were happy, and I was finally home serving God. It was a complete transformation—unbelievable.

Then one day, life as I knew it stopped. It stopped, and I was not sure why. Was God in this? My faith would be tested more than it had ever been.

Last Love, whom I was supposed to have left, was still engraved in my heart. I had called him one day from a payphone. Nobody knew. People would think I was crazy, but I had to hear his voice. I had to know that he was sorry and that this was not the man I knew. He was quiet on the other end of the phone at first, and then he started to cry. He said he was so happy I called and that he was so very sorry. He did not mean to do anything to hurt me. He told me he had been sober since that day. We began talking again without anyone knowing, and as long as he wasn't drinking, I was okay with being around him. He was heartbroken over what had occurred and could not believe he actually hurt me. Last Love thought he could be a two-beer man; he was an alcoholic, and there was no way two beers would be enough. I felt so badly for him. He still had many issues to heal from. We had an understanding beyond physical intimacy—an intense love and friendship. His laughter is what I longed for. I eventually was able to get my own apartment and moved back near our old home. We shared short periods of time together, mostly in secret. Motorcycle rides in the afternoons. One Sunday he actually came into church to say hi to me. He knew my life was different; I talked about all the things God was doing in my life, and I found out one day that he had accepted Jesus too! He was eighteen when his father passed away, and his brother shared Christ's love with him. I told him it was probably time to get his life back on track and go back to living a fulfilled life with Jesus. I stood firm on not being more than friends with him. I had done the opposite too many times to know it was not going to work.

Finally, a good thought pattern, Emily!

Well of course his drinking become worse; he would stay around for short periods, not drinking in front of me, then things would get fumbled in his mind again, and he had to drink. He called during those times and told me to either come home or stay away. One night the hospital called me; I was not going to answer the phone, but thank God I did. He had gotten jumped and was seriously hurt. He had suffered a bad concussion. They asked me to come and pick him up, and they wanted to know if I knew anyone that could stay with him. Of course, I offered to. You knew I would! It was nice to care for him again. At home I made sure he slept well. We lay on the couch together, talked, and enjoyed the time of healing he had.

Last Love was back to normal in two weeks. The neighbors came over when I would walk out to make sure I was okay and that he was good. They told me he has not been the same since I left. They had my back and told me to be careful. I had such a good relationship with God that I felt strong and knew I would be fine. Once he was well enough to go to work, I went back to my apartment. That was hard for him, and I have to admit it was hard for me too.

This off-and-on relationship would occur over the next year and a half.

I stayed strong and faithful in serving God and prayed diligently for Last Love to realize what was happening.

One night he called and asked me for help after about a month of no contact. I explained that I could not come over because he was drinking. He said he was done and needed my help. I reluctantly went over, praying that God would have His way with this moment. Last Love wanted to enter into rehab. I was shocked and filled with disbelief, but he was crying for forgiveness. I would not make the call unless he got on his knees and asked God for forgiveness. Not that I was in charge or anything; I just did not want to make that type of call without knowing he really meant it. He had been drinking; this was not normal behavior for him.

Last Love had told me once again that he was saved when he was eighteen years old and coming out of the service but that he just was not so very faithful. His faith had diminished when his mother died a few years back.

Last Love prayed with me and asked for forgiveness and cried. I know he was heard. God is amazing! Last Love went to rehab for thirty days, and it was amazing to see him sober. His brother and I visited. He looked healthy. I asked him to stay longer, but the stubbornness had not left him yet, and he came home thinking he could handle a few beers from time to time. He still wondered why I would not come home. I explained how he had to be sober and respect me. He would at least have to work on himself for one year as his counselors advised. This was my first lesson with Monte. Last Love, of course, did not like this. It was too hard for him to be alone.

I understood that feeling too well. He begged me over and over again, but I couldn't. God had delivered me from so many things.

It was so difficult for him; his alcoholism won again. It was worse than ever.

One day he was so angry at me for helping my daughter and not being with him that he yelled and told me to stay away for good! I did. I missed him so much and wanted to call but left him completely to God. This time I was not going to rescue him nor answer his calls—not until God intervened. I had no idea that God would physically take him six weeks later.

One of our good friends called me. He had been worried because a few of them had not heard from Last Love in a couple of days. Last Love had even missed work, which was out of character of him. I gave instructions how our friend could get into the house to check things out. Maybe he was just passed out. I waited for my friend to call me as he entered into the house through one of the windows I had told him about.

The date was August 6, 2012. My friend called me screaming, and I got into my car and drove to the Last Love's house. My friend found Last Love dead in the bathtub; Last Love was sitting up and completely clothed. The coroner and police calculated that Last Love had been dead for at least three days.

I cannot explain the heartache I had as I waited for my friend's phone call and then drove to the house and saw my friends face as he exited the house while the police were arriving.

I had remembered my pastor's phone number and called for his help; he came right over and stayed till I had everything settled. No one had all Last Love's phone numbers of his contacts, family, and so forth. That night, I stayed with my daughter Crystal, I cried so much.

I questioned God and His reasoning for actually taking Last Love from me.

Right before I fell asleep, God sent me a sign, one that gave me assurance that He had Last Love with Him. It was a reminder—the smell of Last Love's cologne. I jumped up! I could not believe it as I scooped the air into my nostrils for more!

Thank you, Lord, this will help me sleep.

Life was a little different now. I did not understand why God would do this to me. I was heartbroken for months, almost to the point of taking my own life. There were months of dark depression that followed. Why should I go on? What was my purpose in life? Everything that the Lord had worked with me though had been erased in my mind: all the good, all the miracles. How quickly our mortal human minds and bodies forget just as the twelve who walked with Christ did. They had so many miracles right in front of them, and yet they still forgot the grace and mercies shown upon them when the storms blew through them. But I did not drink!

What was the purpose of living without him? I thought. Why did I feel I needed him? Then suddenly out of nowhere a peace came over me. I realized Last Love was in a much better place and that in all actuality my prayer was heard. God was fully in control and had taken him for his own safety and to help. He had heard Last Love's cries of despair. You see, Last Love could have been asking to go home with the Lord because his pain and inability to stop drinking were too great. No one really knows what those last moments were like for Last Love.

One day, I drove to the mortuary and cried. Questioning my purpose, I prayed for clarity and actually called a Christian radio station for prayer and asked for help in my moment of despair. After praying, I realized my life is still here and that I had a lot more to do. Perhaps I should say God has a lot more for me to do.

You see, He is not finished with me yet!

18

Serious Note

Pretty amazing, isn't it, how things all work out for good?

I do want to take a moment to discuss something very real and very important. I was a lucky lady to take the chance and communicate with Last Love, especially after having a restraining order in place. I do not recommend this at all for anyone. I am not proud I took that route and am very fortunate I made it out alive. Counselors will teach to have a key word—a safe word—that will let others know you need help. I had one friend who I relayed everything to: where I was going and when I was supposed to be home. There are too many women who attempted what I did and did not make it out alive. Do not do anything in secret; let someone you trust know what you are thinking and why. They will help you. This dependence on another human is not healthy, and it will drain the life out of you if you do not get help.

Call a radio station or any medical facility and let them know you are not in a safe place. They are now trained to address your needs.

19

Hallelujah! It Is Healing Time

Emily's storm was long and so very turbulent, although through it she has been blessed in many ways. She, like me, was very broken many times.

If it wasn't for our storms, we would not appreciate all the wonders of Jesus as our savior today.

Through my own personal journey I have hurt many individuals, and I pray that if you as a reader are one of those people who crossed my path, I humbly ask your forgiveness.

Meeting Emily has shown me that through my own pain, God has allowed me to be seasoned with maturity in order to fully accept what he is capable of doing through me.

Like Emily, here I am today able to help abused women and children. I am able to help others to understand the feeling of guilt and low self-worth. Abuse can be physical and mental; it can be soft and quiet at first and then take over your very soul.

Emily completed college; this was the grace and plan the Lord had for her.

In the midst of all the chaos in my own life, He helped me finish college, my teachers' credential program, and my masters in special education. Why? Because that was His plan even before I was born. He knew I would be doing what I am doing, and He knew I was going to take a few little turns. His plan will always prevail no matter how long it seems to take. It took me eighteen years in total to complete my education. Amazing, that is all I can say—our Lord is amazing.

The Lord has blessed me with the wonderful job of caring and a heart for service work. These are only a few of the great gifts He has blessed me with. With these gifts I am able to love His most precious children and young adults whom He entrusts to me every day. All I can say is wow!

Along with Emily, I have learned one hard lesson: if we fill our souls with the word of God and pray with a grateful heart, we should not feel lonely. Do I still get lonely? Yes, I would not be truthful if I told you otherwise. However, I know that I am able to receive new grace daily, and I am grateful for this promise from God. I believe that when God thinks we are ready for a partner, He will send one, but only if we are emotionally secure in serving Him first! Our Lord loves to be the center of attention! As He should. Remember, He plans our day while we are sleeping. We should jump for joy with excitement when we open our eyes!

"What do we get to do today? Lord, help me to see Your plan."

Yes, I am still a work in progress, and praise God for that! Please keep me in your prayers if you remember, and I pray that if you are reading Emily's story, God will reveal His promise to you in order for you to know that, yes, you have a purpose, and God does want you to see it. And, most of all, that you are good enough.

CONCLUSION

Stories of Faith

As with Emily, many of us have a story.

Never in a million years would I think God would use me to write on paper in this way. He has been asking me for over year now, "Don't forget about that book. You need to write that book. Hey, you remember that book? The book I had started over twenty years ago?"

On a personal level I wanted to share a couple of amazing things that God has done for me since beginning my journey as an author.

My life as a single parent had many different turns in it as well; many of which are the same feelings that Emily had. Striving to be good enough, striving to be loved. Sometimes wondering if this was going to be as good as it gets. I dedicated my life to Christ as a young teenager. I went through life making mistakes and learning along the way. Hurting people and realizing that I needed to make changes. These changes, I have learned, could not be made by me alone; they had to be released to God, and He needed to make them through me. A very hard lesson to learn. Let go and let God. My tests in life have become my testimony. When I felt alone and hurt, He was carrying me, waiting for me to reach out to Him.

My desire in life today is to continue to serve, reach for my purpose, the one that has been in His plan since the beginning of time.

Both of my adult girls know the Lord and are learning to love Him every day. My mom and dad started to have a relationship with Christ this past year. You can't imagine how cool it is to call my mom and hear her tell me of all the wonderful things she reads about in the Bible. My mom recently told me she can't believe she waited till she was seventy-five to meet Jesus. Dad is a praying man; he is blind and a diabetic, and he loves God and loves watching me do God's work. Mom and Dad are divorced. Mom asks about Dad, but we still haven't gotten in them same room yet. Some of you may know what that is like.

I have four wonderful grandchildren; the little ones enjoy going to church and singing to God.

Oh, my career is beginning its fifteenth year. Can you believe it?

God answered a prayer of financial freedom and gave me a new home to purchase, zero down, and right down the street from one of my daughters. Wow!

Just like Emily, your prayers have sustained us. Thank you to everyone who prayed for me throughout my life. Those prayers kept me alive—alive enough to hear God's whisper.

Keep strong, don't give up, and do not ever think you're not good enough.

Most of all, remember God does not give up on us. We tend to give up on Him, but He will always be there facing you with His arms stretched out! Take them. Let Him hold you, love you, and take you to the place you are supposed to be.

For those of you who do not know Jesus or know how to meet him, it is a simple prayer of asking God to forgive you of your sins. Let Him know that you know He died on the cross for you and that you want to commit your life to Him in order to have everlasting life. Then find a church or call a Christian radio station near you. Talk to someone and ask them for the next step, get a Bible, and pray. Prayers do not have to be fancy; Jesus likes you to just talk to Him. My pastor told me once that God help is the best prayer ever.

Remember that He will always be there no matter what you do, that you are exactly where you're supposed to be right now, and that you will always be good enough!

Testimony from the Author

Here is one short, amazing story of how God used me.

I am blessed to be able to have the opportunity to share this experience with you.

I am a teacher of moderate to severely disabled high school students. What a blessing every day to be able to care and love God's most precious human beings.

My story begins with a Bible study at our local church. It was the end of the study when the video asked the ladies to stand, hold hands to pray together, and then stand shoulder to shoulder, not allowing anything to get in between us. What a glorious experience as we had been together for the last eight weeks, and standing this close was a great way to end together.

As with many new things God brings to my attention, I saw this as wonderful teaching opportunity. You see, the kids had just started back to school after a long summer break, and for some reason, their reasoning of why they were together in my class had been lost. They had to learn to get along again the way their teacher requires them all to do in her class. I try to always instill the importance of using their talents and God-given gifts to help each other as well as to reach out into the community and give back. The next day I asked all the kids to come outside to our little courtyard. As with most kids with disabilities, they are usually off to the side and away from the main campus. The kids complied, and I asked the adults to join as well. They had a funny look, but then again, they have become accustomed to my off-the-wall tactics at teaching our wonderful kids!

I asked them to hold hands and get into a circle. They did; I asked them how it felt, and they said, "Good." I reminded them that this is how we are to become united and help each other—as one big family. One may not be able to tie their shoes, but another can for him; one may not be able to express his needs verbally, but another will, and so you can get the idea. The students agreed to stop the bickering, and then came the good part! I asked them to stand shoulder to shoulder. The adults looked at me funny again but did as I instructed as did the kids.

I said, "Now this is how close we would be this year!" All agreed and hoorayed.

As we began to walk back into the classroom, one of my students called out to me and said, "Ms. Dauntless?"

"Yes, darling," I replied.

"Why can't we do that out there?" She was referring to the main campus.

"Out there?" I asked.

"Yes."

"Well I never thought of that, but let me see what I can do."

Oh boy, Lord. How am I going to do this? There were 1,500 kids divided up on the campus. This being my second year, I have noticed such a division between the students and the staff. There was just no school spirit—no unity.

I truly can't explain it and can only say that God has me there for a big purpose, and it was beginning to unfold in front of me!

I went home, prayed, and wondered how this would or could happen. Last year the principal would barely talk to me. This year I was blessed with the position of being sophomore class advisor, which gives me an "in," so let's see. I asked him if I could talk to him. I went to his office and said that my kids and I would like to try something big on campus during lunch—we would like to try an activity of unity. He liked it! I later found out he was a believer like me! I went back to class and told my students we would try. They were so excited. I orchestrated an all-staff e-mail with the intent to bring unity to my students and the general education population and asked if anyone would want to be a part of this activity. To my dismay, I received no reply, probably because I was still so new.

So it was just going to be us. I discussed the activity with the cheer coach and her girls. They loved it. Why not, they said, something has to happen! We had a few supporters now! Praise God!

How do I invite 1,500 kids to the middle of the quad at one time, Lord?

God gave me the idea of having my kids personally inviting the students. We made over one thousand small notes with little stickers and colorings from my precious group that only stated, "Meet me at the quad at 12:50." I explained to the kids it was going to be a surprise and that all we had to do was pass all the notes out to as many of the students and staff as we could. We only had brunch to pass out the notes. They agreed excitedly. I sent them out on their way with little baskets, and off they went passing notes all around. I could hear them say, "Can you come to my party?" and "I can't tell, it is a surprise!" Kids were running to get the little notes from my students. It was glorious to watch. One of the teachers asked me what I was going to do when no one shows up and how it was going to be a letdown of great magnitude. I told him, that is where you are wrong. God is amazing, and the kids know my heart. I teach my kids the importance of not giving up. If no one comes, the words that would come out of their mouths would be, "It's okay, Ms. Dauntless, we will try again!" That's my answer with all things.

Don't ever say never because God will make a way if it is in His plan. Amen!

The time was getting close, and the kids were sitting on a table near the quad excitedly. Is it time yet, Ms. Dauntless? Is it time? How much longer? It was like going on a long road trip with your family.

The quad is a large, rounded middle section of the main campus that is concrete. Around it are tables and grass where kids from all backgrounds sit and hang out. No one ever walks through the middle, let alone hang out in the middle.

It is 12:45, and the principal comes by in his little cart and says to us, "Are you ready for shoulder to shoulder?" We said yes and walked out to the middle. There stood thirteen little kids jumping up and down with excitement. Giggling and laughing and looking around, the students were calling out, "Come on! Come on!" I walked over to a few of the tables and asked if they had gotten a note. Clearly they had because they had it in their hands. They looked away as though to tell me who was I to walk up to their domain. I said, "Look, over there, those kids worked really hard to invite you to a small gesture that they want you to be a part of. This isn't for me, it is for them."

It took a leader from each little clique to walk out, and then they called out their groups, giving them the OK to participate. Little by little they walked toward the middle of the campus. I was elated! The kids were excited and greeting them and asking them, "Can you hold our hands?" I was in the middle of this group, and kids were running to be a part of what was unfolding right in front of me! God's wonder! I cannot express how glorious it was. I had tears streaming down my face. I was running around the crowd thanking them.

Soon I looked, and the circle had gotten so large there were over three hundred kids all holding hands, and I was in the middle. Then the wonder grew. I could hear the echo from within the shoulder-to-shoulder gathering. "Get closer. Shoulder to shoulder," they whispered. *Amazing, Lord, You did it! You really did it!* Then it was silent. I was not prepared for such a large crowd, and I had to scream to allow everyone to hear my gratitude. "Thank you!" I expressed over and over again. "Thank you so very much. This is how we need to be close and united!" Then, after a brief moment of silence from the other side of the circle facing toward the middle, one of my students yelled out to me.

"Ms. Dauntless!"

"Yes, darling?" I yelled.

"Is this how many friends we have?"

Now I was crying. "Yes, my love, this is how many friends we have!"

God showed me how amazing He was that day as He did with many other. A couple of the adults told me they didn't think it would happen and that if I thought the sight was amazing from within, I should have seen it from the outside as the kids ran over. Now more than ever I know that God has a plan.

Isn't our God amazing?

My goal, with God by my side, is to bring awareness of how important it is to include my students. People say hi to us all the time, and we went to our first ever high school dance on campus! I know God is going to continue to work wonderful things with us.

Thank you for reading my story, and I hope that it blesses you.

If you remember or ever think of us, pray that God will continue to send me helpers and that God will continue to move in a marvelous way.

¹ Let all that I am praise the LORD;
with my whole heart, I will praise his holy name.

² Let all that I am praise theLORD;
may I never forget the good things he does for me.

³ He forgives all my sins and heals all my diseases.

⁴ He redeems me from death and crowns me with
love and tender mercies.

⁵ He fills my life with good things. My youth is
renewed like the eagle's!

⁶ The LORD gives righteousness and justice to all who
are treated unfairly.

⁷ He revealed his character to Moses and his deeds to
the people of Israel.

⁸ The LORD is compassionate and merciful, slow to
get angry and filled with unfailing love.

⁹ He will not constantly accuse us,
nor remain angry forever.

¹⁰ He does not punish us for all our sins;
he does not deal harshly with us, as we deserve.

¹¹ For his unfailing love toward those who fear him is
as great as the height of the heavens above the earth.

¹² He has removed our sins as far from us as the east
is from the west.

¹³ The LORD is like a father to his children,
tender and compassionate to those who fear him.

¹⁴ For he knows how weak we are;
he remembers we are only dust.

¹⁵ Our days on earth are like grass;
like wildflowers, we bloom and die.

¹⁶ The wind blows, and we are gone—
as though we had never been here.

¹⁷ But the love of the LORD remains forever with
those who fear him. His salvation extends to the
children's children

¹⁸ of those who are faithful to his covenant, of those
who obey his commandments!

¹⁹ The LORD has made the heavens his throne; from
there he rules over everything.

²⁰ Praise the LORD, you angels, you mighty ones
who carry out his plans, listening for each of his
commands.

²¹ Yes, praise the LORD, you armies of angels who
serve him and do his will!

[22] Praise the LORD, everything he has created,
everything in all his kingdom.

Let all that I am praise the LORD.

—Psalm 103:1–22, NLT

Introduction to "Chapter 0"

I would like to tell you how "Chapter 0" came to be part of my book.

Jay was the first person who read about Emily. He had never met her but knew from my words on paper that she had something I needed to share. God's love, a way to forgive. He encouraged me to complete my project.

He personally stated he was able to relate to the many heartaches. He is a loving husband and father and has a deep desire to serve the Lord. He is a freestyle poet and is working on his own book of poetry; with this in mind, I asked him to write a few poems for my book. Each one that was written came from certain defining moments in Emily's story.

Now that you know what inspired me to make these poems part of *Free at Last: The Struggle to Be Good Enough*, I want to share Jay Steel's letter to me, the author, as I believe it will give you a greater insight on the connection.

Dear I. M. Dauntless,

I am sincerely humbled and blessed to be a part of *Free at Last: The Struggle to Be Good Enough.* Emily's story truly touched my heart. Coming from a single-family home and later raising a child as a single parent, I could certainly relate to Emily's great struggle and journey. I suppose you can say that my deep connection with Emily is due to the fact that I have experienced both worlds.

Being raised by my grandmother in a single-parent home really allowed me to find my calling creatively, as I remember spending many days doing various creative things such as drawing, painting, and creating stories. It also taught me how to fend for myself and appreciate what life offers, what God gives you, and the difference between the two. When I became a single parent, the experience that I attained as a child in a single-family home helped me keep my child occupied by doing the same creative things that I did as a child.

Many will be blessed by Emily's story and inspired by her great will to overcome the cards that she was dealt and the strength God gave her.

May God continue to strengthen you as you continue to strengthen others though your amazing stories and faith-filled journey!

Sincerely,
Jay Steel

CHAPTER 0

Excerpts of Poetry from Jay Steel

This is dedicated to the tough, strong, loving, caring, unselfish, unwavering, steadfast, kind, thoughtful, gentle, helpful, considerate, compassionate, concerned, loving, sensitive, affectionate, tender, devoted, adoring, warm, loyal, dedicated, faithful, committed, attentive, supportive, fond, and responsive single parents who work very hard every day and night to ensure the very best for their child's physical and mental well-being. Nothing could ever replace the countless books read; stories told; sleepless nights spent; and/or breakfast, lunches, dinners, and snacks made and delivered. You will truly be rewarded by God's many great blessings as he has made you tough, strong, loving, caring, unselfish, unwavering, steadfast, kind, thoughtful, gentle, helpful, considerate, compassionate, concerned, loving, sensitive, affectionate, tender, devoted, adoring, warm, loyal, dedicated, faithful, committed, attentive, supportive, fond, and responsive for a reason. This last section was inspired by you and dedicated to you! Continue being you!

With much love and the highest respect,
Jay Steel

A TOAST TO ME

Can I be good enough,
good enough for you?
Why do I doubt
the things that I do?

Can all the lies
all be true?
Why do I make up
these lies just for you?

What does it mean
to love and be loved?
When push comes to shove
why do I hug?

Why do I try
to be so close
To good times, bad times
let's make as toast

A toast to the bad
I will take all the blame
No matter how bad
I'll just feel the same

A toast to the good
These times are rare
For me you don't care
so for me I don't care

Don't stop and stare
Just stop and share
The pain and the blame
It has to be fair

They say that nothing
In life is for free
Except for my spirit
And soul, please see

HOW MANY OF US HAVE THEM

Catch me I'm falling
or just let me fall
Send me a letter
or make a quick call

Tell me how valuable
and loved that I am
Tell me I'm good,
I'm good and I can

Lead me to believe,
Believe in myself
Help me put
my doubts on the shelf

Encourage me
to inspire me
Make me see
that I am free

Free from the pain
and anger that hides
Free from the infliction
of ego and pride

Just one more day
to get through again
A cup of coffee
with my great friend

A meeting of the minds
to discuss all the worse
Covering the wounds
without a nurse

Just the Lord
and his almighty words
and support from my friends
when my cries are heard

I WILL TAKE ALL OF THE BLAME FOR IT ALL

I'm on deaths list
Convicted by myself
For leaving life's lessons
On a cold wood shelf

On the lonely road
Few stops along the way
No turning back
Tomorrow's new day

Been there
and I did that
I wore each
and every hat

Been there and
Tried this
Those days
I try to miss

Sometimes I feel sad
Oftentimes I get mad
Sometimes I cry out
Oftentimes I have doubt

Can you feel my sorrow?
Can you see my pain?
Can I be the same person
with all the shame?

It's not my fault
But it was my choice
I'm not that hurt
Cause I still have a voice

Will you please forgive me
For all of your mistakes
Forget about the pain
I caused when you would take

Nothing is alright
Nothing's very fine
Even though my mind is blank
I try to speak my mind

Those sounds in the night
were not the great winds
It was me praying
for forgiveness for my sins

I'M UNTITLED

Please don't scream at me
Please talk nice
Please don't yell at me
It's common sense advice

Please stop all
of your petty this and thats
Please stop all
of your fat chitchat

Let me be myself
Let my soul be free
Why hover over me?
Let me be me

Let me act the way I acted
long before we met
Let me say the things I said
before our love had debt

They say love is blind
They say love's for fools
If Elvis was alive
He would sing, "Don't be cruel"

Don't be the one who
I love to hate
Be the same person
Who I used to date

.

Just because were married
Doesn't mean that we are friends
Just because you act fake
Doesn't mean that it's pretend

Did you forget my name?
You think you have much game
Play it like you never have
or we'll never be the same

MY MEMORY LANE

Let's take a trip
down memory lane
My street of love,
despair, and pain

A street that hides
deep down inside
A place where I
cried, tried, and cried

In a house on my hill
My feelings I spill
Out like a drink
What's fake or for real?

The truth can hurt
Just like a lie
I try and I try
and still don't know why

My babies are crying
What do I do?
No one told me
They knew as they grew

How much more
can we all take?
Lord, please help us
For your Heaven's sake

Because your plan
for us is to live
A much better life
to receive one must give

The trials and hurdles
that life throws your way
Now that I know
I just stay away

Away from the trouble
and hurt that I find
Away from myself
I'm no longer blind

Now the house
on my hill is complete
Now that GOD
He lives on my street

OPEN UP TO CLOSE UP

I'm like a closed book
and my thoughts "Not for sale"
Many try to read
but most often they fail

I sometimes wonder
Why I act the way I do
Why I stick around
And spend time with you

Could it be
I am young and immature
If that's the only problem
I don't need a cure

No prescription to fill
For feeling unalive
No need to call the doctor
I'm done with all the jive

It's time to break free
From the chains that love brings
It's time to be happy
To smile, dance, and sing

We will be okay
We will be alright
Even if my babies
have questions every night

Cuz one day they'll know
How much Mom cares
One day they'll know
That this life's not fair

PARK BENCHES AND PARKING LOTS

Eight million stories
in a naked city
Eight billion souls
in a city of pity

The crime rates high
and so is the mayor
Can you spare some change?
Can you spare some prayers?

It's cold outside
It will soon begin to rain
Graffiti under the bridge
has a new picture frame

Hot tea is on
to warm a cold soul
A result of sex,
drugs, rock 'n' roll

The top has sprung a leak
time to move out!
Load up the cart!
Put the fire out!

I would have lived different
If I would have known how
I can't look back
I have to live now

THE PRAYER PILL

Dr. Everything Is
Going To Be Alright
Said,
"Get the much needed
sleep at night"

Don't sweat the small things
that life can bring
Even though the small things
can sometimes sing

Songs of desperation,
despair and pain
The song could be louder
but remains to be the same

The same as before
Little has changed
The same issues and problems
Just rearranged

Maybe some pills
could help with the math
Something to change
My history's wrath

Doctor, Doctor,
What could it be?
Can you prescribe
a pill to see?

See through the obstacles
in life that we face
See through the people
that will leave a bad taste

See through the doors
as opportunity knocks
The hands never stop
on life's grand clock

No pills like that
come to mind
"That, my friend
would be such a great find

"A pill for you
if I may suggest, my friend
Would be to pray every day
until the end"

YOU AND ME TOGETHER UNTIL TOGETHER IS NO LONGER FOREVER (TIME'S UP)

I hate you as much
as I hate me
Do you really want to grow
this fine family tree?

How could I
just get up and go?
How could I
Just let the world know?

How much you don't
really mean to me
You could mean much more
if you weren't so mean, see

You're an angel from Heaven
when your family is near
and when they leave
we live in fear

Your like Dr. Jekyll
and his friend Mr. Hyde
You have good qualities
but pain hides inside

I try to believe
that you will someday change
But it's just so hard
when you act so strange

I'd take the bad with the good,
but there's not much good
I would walk out the door
if I only could

If I only could
be the perfect one
Would you love me more,
Could this war be done?

If I only could
have the perfect smile
Would you hold me tight
and stay awhile?

If I only could
If I only could
I would shout out loud
You are no good!

No good for you!
No good for me!
We must be blind!
Why can't we see?

You really don't deserve
the chances that I give
so I give up
time to live, live, live!

INTRODUCING THE GREATEST

Step right up
Come one, come all
Listen to the words
Small stand tall

Jesus is alive
Living on HIS Earth
I felt HIS mighty grace
and His presence since birth

His undiscovered gifts
Lie within your heart
Haven't figured it out?
Today's a brand new start

Now is the time
It is never too late
To come to the Lord
and own your own fate

Against all hate
sin and crime
Now is the time,
Now is the time

So close your eyes
and repeat these words
Quiet or loud
proud or unheard

I accept You, Christ
Come into my heart
I make you my Savior
Today I will start

Lord I thank you
for all you have done
The creator of life,
The stars and the sun

You died on the cross
Then rose from the dead
They laughed as you bled
With thorns in your head

Your grace will always
be tested by time
To try to live without it
would destroy all minds

Bodies and souls
Your heart is whole
The perfect gift
With no death toll

Just infinite life
In the Heavens above
Where the angels sing
With white doves in love

An Incredible place
Indescribable to all
Free from the pain
Free from the fall

The fall of all
From all of our sin
The same sin that wins
again and again and again and again

CPSIA information can be obtained
at www.ICGtesting.com
Printed in the USA
BVOW11s2023230916
463064BV00002B/2/P